GAMEPLAN

A Comedy

by Alan Ayckbourn

samuelfrench.co.uk

Copyright © 2002 by Haydonning LTD
All Rights Reserved

GAMEPLAN is fully protected under the copyright laws of the British Commonwealth, including Canada, the United States of America, and all other countries of the Copyright Union. All rights, including professional and amateur stage productions, recitation, lecturing, public reading, motion picture, radio broadcasting, television and the rights of translation into foreign languages are strictly reserved.

ISBN 978-0-573-11567-7
www.samuelfrench.co.uk
www.samuelfrench.com

For Amateur Production Enquiries

United Kingdom and World
excluding North America
plays@samuelfrench.co.uk
020 7255 4302/01

Each title is subject to availability from Samuel French,
depending upon country of performance.

CAUTION: Professional and amateur producers are hereby warned that GAMEPLAN is subject to a licensing fee. Publication of this play does not imply availability for performance. Both amateurs and professionals considering a production are strongly advised to apply to the appropriate agent before starting rehearsals, advertising, or booking a theatre. A licensing fee must be paid whether the title is presented for charity or gain and whether or not admission is charged.

The professional rights in this play are controlled by Casarotto Ramsay Associates, Waverley House, 7-12 Noel Street, London, W1F 8GQ.

No one shall make any changes in this title for the purpose of production. No part of this book may be reproduced, stored in a retrieval system, or transmitted in any form, by any means, now known or yet to be invented, including mechanical, electronic, photocopying, recording, videotaping, or otherwise, without the prior written permission of the publisher. No one shall upload this title, or part of this title, to any social media websites.

The right of Alan Ayckbourn to be identified as author of this work has been asserted in accordance with Section 77 of the Copyright, Designs and Patents Act 1988.

THINKING ABOUT PERFORMING A SHOW?

There are thousands of plays and musicals available to perform from Samuel French right now, and applying for a licence is easier and more affordable than you might think

---

From classic plays to brand new musicals, from monologues to epic dramas, there are shows for everyone.

Plays and musicals are protected by copyright law so if you want to perform them, the first thing you'll need is a licence. This simple process helps support the playwright by ensuring they get paid for their work, and means that you'll have the documents you need to stage the show in public.

Not all our shows are available to perform all the time, so it's important to check and apply for a licence before you start rehearsals or commit to doing the show.

LEARN MORE & FIND THOUSANDS OF SHOWS

Browse our full range of plays and musicals and find out more about how to license a show
www.samuelfrench.co.uk/perform

Talk to the friendly experts in our Licensing team for advice on choosing a show, and help with licensing
plays@samuelfrench.co.uk   020 7387 9373

Acting Editions
BORN TO PERFORM

Playscripts designed from the ground up to work the way you do in rehearsal, performance and study

Larger, clearer text for easier reading

Wider margins for notes

Performance features such as character and props lists, sound and lighting cues, and more

+ CHOOSE A SIZE AND STYLE TO SUIT YOU

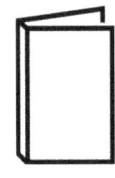

STANDARD EDITION

Our regular paperback book at our regular size

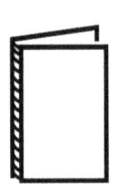

SPIRAL-BOUND EDITION

The same size as the Standard Edition, but with a sturdy, easy-to-fold, easy-to-hold spiral-bound spine

LARGE EDITION

A4 size and spiral bound, with larger text and a blank page for notes opposite every page of text. Perfect for technical and directing use

| LEARN MORE | samuelfrench.co.uk/actingeditions

**Other plays by ALAN AYCKBOURN
published by Samuel French**

Absent Friends

Absurd Person Singular

Arrivals and Departures

Awaking Beauty

Bedroom Farce

Body Language

Callisto 5

The Champion of Paribanou

A Chorus of Disapproval

Comic Potential

Communicating Doors

Confusions

A Cut in the Rates

Dreams from a Summer House

Drowning on Dry Land

Ernie's Incredible Illucinations

Family Circles

Farcicals

FlatSpin

Gizmo

Haunting Julia

Henceforward

Hero's Welcome

House & Garden

How the Other Half Loves

If I Were You

Improbable Fiction

Intimate Exchanges, Volume I

Intimate Exchanges, Volume II

It Could Be Any One of Us

Joking Apart

The Jollies

Just Between Ourselves

Life and Beth

Life of Riley

Man of the Moment

Mixed Doubles

Mr. A's Amazing Maze Plays

Mr Whatnot

My Very Own Story

My Wonderful Day

Neighbourhood Watch

The Norman Conquests: Table Manners; Living Together; Round and Round the Garden

Private Fears in Public Places

Relatively Speaking

The Revengers' Comedies

RolePlay

Roundelay

Season's Greetings

Sisterly Feelings

A Small Family Business

Snake in the Grass

Suburban Strains

Sugar Daddies

Taking Steps

Ten Times Table

Things We Do for Love

This Is Where We Came In

Time and Time Again

Time of My Life

Tons of Money (revised)

Way Upstream

Wildest Dreams

Wolf at the Door

Woman in Mind

A Word from Our Sponsor

FIND PERFECT PLAYS TO PERFORM AT
www.samuelfrench.co.uk/perform

ABOUT THE AUTHOR

Alan Ayckbourn has worked in theatre as a playwright and director for over fifty years, rarely if ever tempted by television or film, which perhaps explains why he continues to be so prolific. To date he has written more than 79 plays, many one act plays and a large amount of work for the younger audience. His work has been translated into over 35 languages, is performed on stage and television throughout the world and has won countless awards.

Major successes include: *Relatively Speaking, How the Other Half Loves, Absurd Person Singular, Bedroom Farce, A Chorus of Disapproval,* and *The Norman Conquests.* In recent years, there have been revivals of *Season's Greetings* and *A Small Family Business* at the National theatre, in the West End *Absent Friends, A Chorus of Disapproval, Relatively Speaking* and *How the Other Half Loves*. In 2015, Chichester mounted a very successful revival of *Way Upstream.*

Artistic Director of the Stephen Joseph theatre from 1972 – 2009 where almost all his plays have been first staged, he continues to direct his latest new work there. In recent years, he has been inducted into American Theatre's Hall of Fame, received the 2010 Critics' Circle Award for Services to the Arts and became the first British playwright to receive both Olivier and Tony Special Lifetime Achievement Awards. He was knighted in 1997 for services to the theatre.

Image credit: Andrew Higgins.

AUTHOR'S NOTE

After a lifetime of playwriting (I first started as an unpublished writer at the age of ten!) my career has moved steadily forward from the status of untried tyro through to establishment figure to ageing experimentalist!

The work has reflected this. From the early tried and tested plays, (*Relatively Speaking, How the Other Half Loves, The Norman Conquests*, etc.) which thankfully people still seem happy to produce and come to see, through the middle period, larger scale so called "social" pieces (*Man of the Moment, A Chorus of Disapproval*) to the more recent smaller scale departures such as *Private Fears in Public Places, Snake in the Grass* and *Haunting Julia*, I have continued to experiment with shape and form, whilst I hope continuing to deepen my characters.

Throughout this, though, I have always needed to remind myself of the overriding prime directive drummed into me at an early age by my mentor, Stephen Joseph, that above all else a playwright is a storyteller.

To keep an audience in their seats you need to involve them in a constantly unfolding series of unexpected twists and turns. These can, of course, be the narrative of the story itself as in *Relatively Speaking* or, as with *Woman in Mind* say, through the psychological development of the characters.

One of the nicest things people can ever say to me, coming out of a new play for the first time of seeing it, is "Well, I never saw THAT coming!"

Alan Ayckbourn

GAMEPLAN

First performed at the Stephen Joseph Theatre, Scarborough, on 29 May 2001. The same production was subsequently presented by Michael Codron, Lee Dean, Michael Linnit, David Ian for ClearChannel Entertainment and Andrew Lloyd Webber, at the Duchess Theatre, London, on 7 September 2002. The cast was as follows:

LYNETTE SAXON	Jacqueline King
SORREL SAXON	Saskia Butler
KELLY BUTCHER	Alison Pargeter
LEO TYLER	Robert Austin
DAN ENDICOTT	Tim Faraday
GRACE PAGE	Beth Tuckey
TROY STEPHENS	Bill Champion

Directed by Alan Ayckbourn
Designed by Roger Glossop
Lighting design by Mick Hughes
Costume design by Christine Wall

CHARACTERS

SORREL SAXON – a schoolgirl, sixteen
LYNETTE SAXON – her mother, a former businesswoman, forty
KELLY BUTCHER – Sorrel's friend, a schoolgirl, sixteen
LEO TYLER – a retired dry-cleaner, forties
DAN ENDICOTT – a police detective sergeant, forties
GRACE PAGE – a WPC, thirties
TROY STEPHENS – tabloid journalist, thirties

The action of the play takes place in a riverside apartment in London's Docklands.

ACT I
Scene One   November, 6 a.m.
Scene Two   The same evening, 6 p.m.
Scene Three   A week later, early afternoon

ACT II
Scene One   The same evening, 11 p.m.
Scene Two   A fortnight later, 6 p.m.
Scene Three   Three weeks later, 4 p.m.

Time – the present

ACT I

Scene One

A riverside apartment on the Thames, somewhere in London's Docklands.

A main sitting area and an adjoining walk-through kitchen/dining area. Sliding windows at one end of the sitting area lead on to a small riverside balcony. At the other end of this sitting area, an understocked bar. Near the window, a desk and chair. A sofa, an armchair and a heavy coffee table. A few quite healthy pot plants dotted around. Leading off this area is a short hallway leading directly to the front door. Also two archways leading to another area visible to us, the common kitchen/dining space. The kitchen end is tidy and well equipped, evidently regularly cleaned. The other end has a small dining table with four chairs. Leading from this is a further door to the offstage bedrooms.

It is 6 a.m. on a cold late-November morning, not yet daylight.

The room is lit by the soft yellow glow of sodium lights reflected from the river.

After a moment, **LYNETTE**, *a woman in her early forties, enters from the bedroom. She has evidently recently awoken. Although already dressed in sweater, jeans and trainers, she's still half-asleep. She is tired, rundown and all in all not in the best of health.*

She goes straight to the kitchen, lifts the kettle to check it has water and switches it on. She finds a mug and primes it with a tea bag. The effort of this has set her off in a fit of coughing.

LYNETTE *(recovering from this first bout)* Oh, God...

This seems to set her off again. She looks towards the bedroom and, trying to muffle the cough, goes to the windows, grabbing her bag on the way. She slides them open and steps on to the balcony. She half-closes the door behind her. Eventually the coughing fit subsides.

(eyes watering) Oh, dear God.

She clutches her chest and takes a few recuperative deep breaths. More or less recovered, she opens her bag and takes out a packet of cigarettes. She lights up and takes a deep drag. She starts another fit of coughing. Eventually she stops again and takes another drag.

Her daughter SORREL, *aged sixteen, comes out of the bedroom, still in her pyjamas. She looks round blearily, awoken by the coughing but not immediately locating her mother. She sees* LYNETTE *and shakes her head in disbelief. She crosses to the window and opens it.*

SORREL *(in exasperation)* Mum, what do you think you're doing?

LYNETTE Oh, darling, I didn't wake you, did I?

SORREL Will you put that cigarette out at once, please?

LYNETTE Oh, come on, this is only my first.

SORREL I should hope so, it's only six o'clock.

LYNETTE I didn't mean to wake you, go back to bed.

SORREL You promised me again last night that you'd stop.

LYNETTE I will. I'm going to. I can't stop just like that, though, can I? I read somewhere that can be just as bad for you, stopping suddenly, as it is to carry on smoking forty a day.

SORREL Where the hell did you read that?

LYNETTE You go back to bed.

SORREL Have you had any tea?

LYNETTE I'm just making some.

SORREL I'll do it. *(She moves to the kitchen)* It's freezing out there, come in. You'll get pneumonia as well. Mothers! Who needs them?

LYNETTE *(coming back into the room)* I was trying not to wake you, that's all.

SORREL *(starting to make them both tea)* If you don't want to wake me then don't stand out there coughing yourself to death outside my bedroom window.

LYNETTE This is the last one I'm having this morning.

SORREL *(unimpressed)* Great.

LYNETTE I don't know why you don't go back to bed. You don't need to get up for another hour.

SORREL I'll do some revision.

LYNETTE You were up until God knows when. What time did you come to bed?

SORREL About two.

LYNETTE Sorrel, four hours sleep isn't enough.

SORREL It's enough for you, apparently.

LYNETTE I'm older. I don't need sleep. You'll collapse. What were you doing till two o'clock, anyway?

SORREL Nothing. Just on the internet, that's all.

LYNETTE Well, I hope it was nothing – you know...

SORREL What?

LYNETTE You know. Like that.

SORREL Oh, come on, Mum. I'm sixteen, for God's sake. It was just a chat room, that's all.

She brings the two mugs of tea to the table.

Here you are.

LYNETTE Thanks. Chat rooms. I don't know what people find to talk about…

She sits at the table with her mug. She takes a mirror from her bag and studies herself.

SORREL *stands and watches her, sipping her own tea as she does so.*

SORREL I wouldn't bother, you look terrible.

LYNETTE Thank you.

She stares at herself without enthusiasm, jabs at her hair with her fingers and then gives up and puts away the mirror.

SORREL Were you serious last night?

LYNETTE Mmm?

SORREL Were you serious? About us having to move?

LYNETTE We can't afford to live here much longer, that's for sure.

SORREL Where will we go?

LYNETTE We'll find somewhere.

SORREL Where?

LYNETTE Somewhere less expensive than here. I don't know. Maybe even out of London.

SORREL *(outraged)* Out of London?

LYNETTE Possibly. Property's much cheaper once you get—

SORREL What about school?

LYNETTE Well, you may have to commute, I don't know—

SORREL Commute? Where from, Birmingham?

LYNETTE Don't be silly. We all have to make sacrifices. That's the price we pay.

SORREL All except Dad.

LYNETTE What?

SORREL Hell of a lot of sacrifices he's made.

LYNETTE *(muted)* Don't start on that again.

SORREL Sunning himself on some bloody beach with that woman.

LYNETTE Please, Sorrel, that's enough...

SORREL I hope he gets skin cancer...

LYNETTE Sorrel!

SORREL I hope they both do.

LYNETTE Don't say that, even as a joke.

SORREL I'm not joking. I hate him. The bastard. I hate him for what he's done to us. To you.

LYNETTE We were probably both to blame, I don't know...

SORREL *(outraged)* How can you both be to blame? How can you say that?

LYNETTE All right, Sorrel! That will do!

SORREL Our business folds, he does nothing, you nearly collapse with stress and he runs off with your partner. Terrific. Thanks so much, Father.

LYNETTE is crying softly.

(contritely) Sorry.

LYNETTE I don't want you to get like this. Please promise me you won't get like this.

SORREL How do you mean?

LYNETTE All...bitter and....vengeful. It's negative. It's pointless. All it hurts in the end is yourself.

SORREL I'll try not to be. Just promise me one thing, though...

LYNETTE What?

SORREL If you ever see me getting seriously involved with a man, that you'll shoot me first.

LYNETTE I've told you. Forget all about Dad. We start again. You and me. New life. Fresh start.

SORREL And you're not even trying to get money out of him?

LYNETTE We don't know where he is.

SORREL Do you think he'll ever get in touch again?

LYNETTE I wouldn't. Maybe for you, he might. Maybe he'll want to see you again.

SORREL Me? He didn't even like me.

LYNETTE Oh yes, he did.

SORREL Anyway, he owes us something.

LYNETTE He hasn't got any money, either. We lost the lot, didn't we?

SORREL It was so quick.

LYNETTE These things are. One minute you've – millions. On paper, anyway – well, not even on paper – on screen. And the next minute...

SORREL Bloody dead loss dot com. Dot utter disaster com.

LYNETTE We weren't the only ones. And there'll be lots more.

Pause.

I'm sorry I shouted at you last night. I was just tired.

She coughs and by reflex reaches into her bag for another cigarette.

SORREL *(warning)* No...

LYNETTE Oh, come on! This is only my sec—

SORREL *(fiercely)* NO!

> **LYNETTE** *hesitates.*

Mum, if you light that cigarette, I warn you I will, I really will walk out and I swear I won't come back. I refuse to sit around here and watch you slowly kill yourself, OK?

> **LYNETTE** *has another small coughing fit but puts away the cigarette, reluctantly.*

Oh, what's the point? You'll light up as soon as you're out the front door, won't you?

LYNETTE No, I won't. I can be strong-willed if I want to be. *(She looks at her watch)* I'd better go.

SORREL Seriously. What are we going to do? We can't carry on like this.

LYNETTE We'll manage.

SORREL We are clearly not, though, are we? We're going to have to move, we've got no money. You haven't even got a proper job. I may finish up moving schools, God knows where we'll go—

LYNETTE I've told you, you are not moving schools.

SORREL It may come to that, mightn't it? We certainly can't afford to live round here any more.

LYNETTE And I have got a proper job.

SORREL What? Temporary office cleaner?

LYNETTE It's a perfectly good job. Hundreds of people—

SORREL Working twelve hours a day?

LYNETTE Nonsense. Dozens of—

SORREL Getting paid next to nothing?

LYNETTE Sorrel, don't be such a snob. It's a perfectly decent job. Lots of people do it!

SORREL Mum, you used to *run* offices, now you're cleaning them.

LYNETTE Times change, don't they? *(She gets up)* I'll see you this evening.

She gets her coat from the hallway and starts to put it on during the following.

SORREL And you still won't let me help?

LYNETTE What do you mean?

SORREL What I said last night. I'm perfectly prepared to try and get a job. Part-time. Help bring in some money—

LYNETTE Sorrel, we talked this to death—

SORREL We shouted it to death. I could manage both, easily—

LYNETTE Forget it. You have wonderful prospects. You're not jeopardising those because of all this. Otherwise it'll all have been for nothing, don't you see? As far as I'm concerned, my life will have been for nothing. Pointless. You're all that matters to me now, Sorrel. And if you want me to be happy, darling, if you care for me in the least little bit, then you will carry on with your life and fulfil all that promise. I will not let you throw it away now. Just because I made a stupid mistake, I refuse to allow it to affect you. That is not going to happen, do you hear me? So, please, let's not talk about it again.

SORREL *is silent.*

See you later, then.

SORREL Yeah. I love you.

LYNETTE *(coming and hugging her)* Love you too. Bye.

SORREL Bye.

LYNETTE *opens the front door.*

And if you love me in the least little bit, then please do not smoke!

LYNETTE *(going, wearily)* Yeah, yeah, yeah...

LYNETTE *closes the door behind her.*

SORREL *stands for a moment, thoughtfully. She goes to the desk and retrieves her own bag. She rummages in it and takes out her mobile. She punches up a pre-dialled number. As she waits for a reply she clears both the mugs to the sink.*

SORREL *(getting a reply)* Hi...yes. Get dressed and come down... No, now... I know it is... I know it is...because I need to talk to you... Listen, if you're my friend, Kell, you'll come down...*now*. Yes.

She disconnects. She rinses the mugs and dries them. She seems to be rehearsing something to herself under her breath, perhaps what she is about to say when her visitor arrives.

The doorbell rings.

SORREL *goes to the door and her friend* **KELLY**, *about the same age, enters.* **KELLY** *is generally slightly in awe of* **SORREL**, *maybe just the tiniest bit in love with her. She has evidently got dressed in a hurry. She wears the school uniform and carries her backpack.*

Come in.

KELLY It's twenty past six.

SORREL Yes, I know.

KELLY Twenty past six. I've never been up at twenty past six in my whole life.

SORREL Welcome to the real world, I'm just going to get dressed.

SORREL *goes off to the bedroom, leaving* **KELLY** *to close the front door.*

KELLY Where are we going?

SORREL *(offstage)* Nowhere. I need to talk.

KELLY Couldn't we have talked on the way to school?

SORREL *(offstage)* It's not that sort of talk. It's private.

KELLY Is it about Jonathan Jacobs, is it?

SORREL *(offstage)* No, it's not about bloody Jonathan Jacobs, thank you very much. I told you he is buried. Seriously buried. I don't want to see him ever again. Ever.

KELLY *(wistfully)* I wouldn't mind him.

SORREL *(offstage)* You're welcome to him, Kelly. He is a jerk and a duplicitous slob, I warn you. And nobody two-times me, I can tell you that.

KELLY goes into the kitchen and helps herself from the fridge.

KELLY *(as she does so, to herself with quiet relish)* Duplicitous slob! *(She calls)* Can I take a Coke?

SORREL *(offstage)* Help yourself.

KELLY Did you finish the essay?

SORREL *(offstage)* Yes.

KELLY I haven't.

SORREL *(offstage)* Then you are in trouble, aren't you, kiddo?

KELLY Probably. It's easy for you.

She locates the biscuit tin.

SORREL *(offstage)* Why didn't you finish it?

KELLY I don't know. I was watching something – on television.

SORREL *(offstage)* Then you are a lazy, idle bitch, Kelly Butcher.

KELLY Probably. *(Her mouth full of biscuit)* Can I have a biscuit?

SORREL *(offstage)* Help yourself.

ACT I, SCENE ONE

> KELLY *wanders back into the sitting-room as* SORREL *enters from her bedroom, finishing dressing in an identical uniform to* KELLY'*s.* SORREL, *though, wears a prefect's badge.*

KELLY I'm late again this month.

SORREL Are you? *(She goes into the kitchen and also helps herself to a can)*

KELLY That's the second time it's happened.

SORREL You can't be pregnant.

KELLY *(gloomily)* I certainly can't. I haven't been with anybody.

SORREL Give it time, kiddo. It'll all happen, I promise. You'll be fighting them off.

KELLY You think so?

SORREL Yeah. What's your hurry?

KELLY I'd just like to – get it over with. Then I can get on with the rest of my life, really.

SORREL It's not all that great.

KELLY No?

SORREL The earth's never moved for me.

> *Pause. They sit and drink.*

KELLY What did you want, then?

SORREL Listen, I'm in all sorts of trouble, really.

KELLY I know you are. How's your mum?

SORREL She's not good. She's pretending – for me – but she's not at all. She's smoking too much. She's had trouble sleeping, so now she's on pills. I'm always catching her crying – that's when we're not screaming at each other. It's all horrible.

KELLY *(sympathetically)* 'Dear. I wish I could do something.

Silence.

No news of your dad, then?

SORREL He's run off, Kelly, hasn't he? How are we going to get news of him? They're hardly going to send us a postcard, are they?

KELLY You think they're abroad?

SORREL Knowing him, yes. Him and that – woman. How can you do that to someone? How can one woman do that to another one? Her so-called friend? Take her husband away like that?

KELLY My mum took my dad away from someone else.

SORREL I just hate sex sometimes.

KELLY I don't know, I've never tried it.

SORREL It's the cause of all the trouble.

KELLY So what's going to happen, then? With you?

SORREL Well, apparently we're going to have to move because we can't afford to live here any longer and consequently I'll have to leave school as, apart from everything else, my mother's health will very probably break down completely and I'll finish up having to nurse her for the rest of my life.

KELLY *(shocked)* That won't happen, surely?

SORREL It might.

KELLY I hope you don't have to leave.

SORREL So do I.

KELLY I'd miss you terribly.

SORREL Yes, well.

KELLY Since Katie Roberts left you're my only real friend now, you know.

SORREL Yes. You are my friend, aren't you?

KELLY Of course. I said.

SORREL And you'd do anything for me, wouldn't you?

KELLY *(a little cautiously)* Yes. Mostly.

SORREL No, Kelly. Not mostly. If you're my real friend, my truly deepest friend, you'd do anything. Anything. You see?

KELLY All right. *(She pauses)* You don't want me to die, do you?

SORREL No, of course I don't. Don't be stupid.

KELLY I thought you might be planning a suicide pact or something.

SORREL I need your help. A good deal of help, you see?

KELLY I don't have any money. I mean, I have my building society account which Auntie Jenny started but I don't think it would be enough to – I mean, if I did have enough you could have it but I don't have that much.

SORREL Look, I don't want money. All I want is help. Just listen a minute, will you? Listen.

KELLY Sorry.

SORREL Do you remember Angela Bletchley?

KELLY *(puzzled)* Angela—?

SORREL She was in the sixth form when we were juniors...

KELLY Oh! You mean Big Angie... Yes. Wasn't she the one who—?

SORREL Got expelled, right. Do you remember why?

KELLY For – sleeping with people, wasn't it?

SORREL Not just sleeping with people. She was charging for it.

KELLY I remember there was talk at the time. I wonder what ever happened to her.

SORREL She's still charging.

KELLY No! I don't believe it! How do you know?

SORREL Because I traced her. I got hold of her old address from one of her friends and I tracked her from there.

KELLY Why on earth did you do that?

SORREL She's amazingly successful. Got this lovely flat. Much nicer than this one.

KELLY Yes, but what does she have to do to get it, Sorrel? Can you imagine it? All those different men? All those strangers you don't know anything about? Ugggh! *(She shivers)*

SORREL It's not like that at all. As a matter of fact, they're not really strangers. She has quite a select list of clients. She's very choosy.

KELLY *(doubtfully)* Well, I wouldn't want to do it. *(She pauses)* Why are we talking about Angela Bletchley? Why did you go and see her?

SORREL Because I wanted to ask her advice.

KELLY Advice?

SORREL On how to go about it.

Silence. KELLY *stares at her incredulously as the penny drops.*

KELLY You're not?

Pause.

You're not?

Pause.

You can't.

SORREL No?

KELLY *gets up and walks about.*

KELLY *(increasingly agitated)* You're going to...you want to...with...just let them...give them...you *can't*.

SORREL Why not?

KELLY Because you can't, Sorrel. It would be wrong. I couldn't bear to think of you doing that. It makes me ill to think about it. You doing that.

SORREL It wouldn't be that bad.

KELLY How could you bear to do it?

SORREL I'd just think about something else, wouldn't I? It wouldn't worry me that much. As I say, I don't think sex is all that great, anyway. It's not going to spoil anything for me.

KELLY God! There must be another way, there must.

SORREL I'd only do it till I'd earned enough money. Then I'd stop.

KELLY I've read they all start out saying that. But most of them in the end, they can't stop. They get addicted.

SORREL That's only when they do drugs as well. I'm not doing drugs.

KELLY Please, Sorrel. There must be something else you can do. Not this.

SORREL What else? I've no qualifications, have I? Not yet.

KELLY What about a newspaper round or something?

SORREL Great! Can you see me earning the sort of money we need from a newspaper round?

KELLY There must be something else.

SORREL Kelly, the sort of money I can earn doing this – it's massive. You should see Angie's flat. She's rolling in it. She says it's money for old rope. It really is.

KELLY But don't you have to – you know – do peculiar things to them? The men. If they ask you?

SORREL *(knowledgeably)* No. Not if you don't want to. Depends what line you go into, of course. I mean, Angie, she's a dominatrix. I'd be straight vanilla, of course.

KELLY Be what?

SORREL Vanilla. That's what they call straight sex. Vanilla. As opposed to, say, S&M or BDSM, or Animal Training or Water Sports or Adults Babies, say.

KELLY How do you know all this?

SORREL Get on the internet, Kell. Your eyes will he opened, girl.

KELLY I can't open anything on my machine. I've still got Net Nanny on mine.

SORREL Oh, come on. You bypass that, don't you?

KELLY I can't.

SORREL God, Kell. No wonder you're still a virgin. Honestly.

Pause.

KELLY So you're seriously going to go ahead with this?

SORREL Yes.

KELLY Where?

SORREL Here.

KELLY In this flat? What about your mum?

SORREL She's at work from six a.m. till six p.m.

KELLY What about the evenings?

SORREL I'll operate daytimes. You can do it in the daytime as well, Kelly. It is allowed.

KELLY What about school?

SORREL I wouldn't do it every day. Then there's the holidays. Plenty of time, then.

KELLY You've really thought it through, haven't you? How are you going to – I mean, you know, get people?

SORREL Clients?

KELLY You're not going to just walk up and down outside, are you?

SORREL For God's sake, Kelly. Internet. Advertise there. Angie showed me one or two reputable sites. All you give is a phone number.

KELLY This phone number? But what if—

SORREL A separate phone number, Kelly. On a mobile. Not even my own mobile. A separate mobile. Business calls only. Miracle of modem technology.

KELLY *(staring at her)* I just don't know what to say. I don't. I thought I knew you. You're my friend. I don't know you at all. Not at all.

SORREL *(smiling)* Well. Urgent needs – desperate measures.

KELLY *(a thought dawning)* And what do you want me to do? Cover for you at school?

Pause.

You don't want me to – I mean you're not planning on – you know, with three of us, are you?

SORREL I wouldn't ask you to do that, Kell. No, I need you to be my maid.

KELLY *(blankly)* Your maid?

SORREL Angie said I should have one. Particularly when I'm starting out. Just in case of – you know, difficulties.

KELLY Difficulties? What difficulties?

SORREL Someone who can open the door and offer them a drink while they're waiting and yell for help if need be.

KELLY I can't do that.

SORREL Yes, you can. Of course you can. Look, it's either you or my mother and I don't think she'd be particularly keen. Quite apart from the fact that she'd be coughing all over the clients, so it's got to be you, Kelly.

KELLY *(in panic)* I can't do that. If my mum found out, she'd go crazy.

SORREL *(fiercely)* Kelly! You promised me you would do anything, remember?

KELLY Yes, but—

SORREL Anything I asked. Remember?

KELLY Yes, but I didn't know you meant this.

SORREL Friendship doesn't come with pre-conditions, Kelly. And if you want to stay my friend you will help me, you hear? I mean it, Kelly.

KELLY *sits miserably. She starts to cry a little.*

Don't start that. Kelly!

KELLY *(through her tears)* I can't be a maid. I've got nothing to wear. What am I going to wear?

SORREL Well, we'll have to go shopping, won't we? Come on, you love shopping up West. There's several shops.

KELLY What, you mean those…weird shops?

SORREL No. Just underwear and things. And…other items. I may have to borrow a little bit from you, Kell.

KELLY What other items?

SORREL You know. Condoms. We'll need condoms. Masses of those.

KELLY I'm not buying condoms.

SORREL Kelly!

KELLY What if a friend of my parents sees me?

SORREL What would a friend of your parents be doing in a sex shop?

KELLY No, true. They're all a bit past that.

SORREL Precisely. So. Are you game? To coin a phrase.

KELLY *(unhappily)* I suppose.

SORREL Cheer up. You'll get a cut.

KELLY A cut.

SORREL A percentage of my earnings. As my maid. Anything I make, you'll get a small share.

KELLY That'll make me a pimp, then. I could go to prison.

SORREL You won't be a pimp. Maybe a Madam. But you've always been that, haven't you?

KELLY How much are you going to charge?

SORREL I'm still working that out. I'll have a sliding scale depending on...on what we...how much they...on the time. Depending. I'm basing it on what Angie told me, though obviously I won't be charging as much as she does. Not to start with. I mean, she's an experienced professional. Whereas I'm really just starting out, aren't I? I mean, it's not that I haven't got some experience, but that was...

KELLY *(softly)* Amateur.

SORREL If you like. OK? *(She holds out her hand to* KELLY*)* Shake on it?

KELLY *reluctantly takes* SORREL*'s hand, then on the spur of the moment hugs her emotionally.*

Come on. Don't be like that. It'll be a laugh.

KELLY A laugh? Making love to strange men?

SORREL In the words of the old song, Kell, what's love got to do with it?

KELLY You'll still be lying there touching them...

SORREL Listen, when we did *Romeo and Juliet* at the end of last term, I had to lie in bed and pretend to make love to David Astwick. David Astwick! Can you imagine? Nothing could be worse than that, I promise you. Come on, let's start walking. I need some air.

She takes up the empty Coke cans and heads into the kitchen.

KELLY So do I.

SORREL I'll just get my scarf. Tell you what. If you show me that essay later I'll try and help you finish it, if you like.

KELLY *(intensely grateful)* Would you really?

SORREL *(smiling at her)* 'Course I would. I'm your friend, aren't I?

KELLY *(in a moment of great happiness)* Yes.

SORREL goes off to the bedroom.

KELLY comes down to reality again.

(to herself) My God, Sorrel! I hope you know what you're doing.

She waits unhappily.

The lights fade to blackout.

Scene Two

The same day, evening. Around six p.m.

LYNETTE *is bustling around in the kitchen making early preparations for their frozen supper. She looks tired and worn after a long day. She pauses in her preparations. Looks at her watch, goes for her bag on the table and gets out her cigarettes. Guiltily she goes on to the balcony and lights one.*

From the river, the sound of a party boat passing. Loud beat music and laughter. **LYNETTE** *watches.*

Consequently she does not hear the front door open cautiously or see **SORREL**'s *exploratory head poke round it.* **SORREL** *sees her mother and darts into the flat with several unmarked carrier bags – which she deposits behind the bar. She nips back and collects a second load. She does the same with these, finally returning to the door to gather up her backpack. She closes the front door, causing* **LYNETTE** *to turn, see her and hastily drop her cigarette over the balcony.*

SORREL *(casually)* Hi!

LYNETTE You're late, aren't you?

SORREL Sorry. I went up West with Kelly.

LYNETTE What doing?

SORREL Just looking round the shops, you know. It was late-night shopping so we thought we'd—

LYNETTE Oh, God. You haven't been spending money, Sorrel?

SORREL No.

LYNETTE We can't afford it, darling. We really can't. Not like we used to.

SORREL I can still look, though, can't I? I'm still allowed to look.

LYNETTE I suppose.

SORREL We went on the tube. Not even a taxi.

LYNETTE I should hope not. I'm just fixing supper. It won't be long. Can you lay the table?

SORREL Sure.

They go about their respective tasks.

LYNETTE Have a good day?

SORREL It was all right.

LYNETTE Get that essay in?

SORREL Yep.

LYNETTE Did Kelly finish hers?

SORREL I finished it for her.

LYNETTE Really! What on earth's the point of that?

SORREL I'm her friend.

LYNETTE It's not going to help her, though, is it? Not in the long run. If you're going to do all her work for her.

SORREL She'd have got into trouble, otherwise. What sort of friend would I have been then?

LYNETTE What were you doing in the West End? What shops did you go in?

SORREL *(vaguely)* All sorts. Selfridges, John Lewis. You know.

LYNETTE See anything nice?

SORREL No. How many cigarettes have you smoked today?

LYNETTE Considerably less than usual.

SORREL God, only forty-five. Hooray.

LYNETTE No. Less than that. And I've never smoked forty-five. Even at my worst.

SORREL You just lose count...

LYNETTE I tell you who I had lunch with, though. Diana Reece. Remember her? She's sold the boutique and she's thinking of opening a gift shop. She wondered if I'd be interested. You know, working there as manager. Once she gets it open.

SORREL Great.

LYNETTE Of course, it wouldn't be for a month or two. Well, probably the middle of next year.

SORREL By which time we'll be living in Carlisle.

LYNETTE I'm trying, Sorrel, I am trying.

SORREL Sorry.

LYNETTE Mind you, you're right. It's probably nothing. Diana's a walking disaster. Everything she touches. Still, I have got us one treat.

She produces a bottle of white wine from the fridge.

I couldn't resist. It was a special offer. We can have a glass of wine with our lasagne.

SORREL Great.

LYNETTE In fact, why don't we have a glass now? Cheer us up, won't it? Now where's the corkscrew? Oh, yes.

SORREL *(in vain)* I'll get it...

But **LYNETTE** *has marched to the bar before* **SORREL** *can stop her.*

LYNETTE God knows what it'll be like. Probably taste like vinegar but if we— *(Seeing* **SORREL***'s collection of carriers)* What's all this?

SORREL *(casually)* Nothing.

LYNETTE I thought you said you didn't buy anything?

SORREL I didn't.

LYNETTE Then where did these come from?

SORREL They're...Kelly's.

LYNETTE Kelly's?

SORREL Yes.

LYNETTE Then what are they doing here?

SORREL I said I'd hide them for her. She went a bit mad. Kept buying things. She said her father'd hit the roof if she arrived home with all this.

LYNETTE I wouldn't blame him.

SORREL Her parents are terribly strict with her, poor kid.

LYNETTE Well, they're a dreadful couple, both of them. No wonder Kelly's such a wimp.

SORREL She's not really. She's just shy, that's all.

LYNETTE Can't think what you see in her.

SORREL Yes, OK. Anyway, I said I'd hide those for her so that she can sneak them in a bit at a time.

LYNETTE I mean, let's face it, she's fearfully dim, isn't she? She must drive you potty.

SORREL I like her. *(She indicates the bottle)* Do you want me to open that?

LYNETTE Please, would you? *(She looks at the carriers)* Well, what are we going to do with all these? We can't leave them here.

SORREL I'll put them in my bedroom.

LYNETTE If you can find room.

SORREL There's room, there's room. Less of that.

LYNETTE When I looked in the other day, it was like a rubbish tip.

SORREL Well, in future, kindly refrain from looking in, please. I have told you that is my private space. What I get up to in there is my own business.

LYNETTE Certainly is. Providing you don't bring anybody else back it is, anyway.

SORREL Would I do that, Mother?

A mobile phone rings.

LYNETTE Whose is that?

SORREL Mine.

LYNETTE You've changed the ring.

SORREL Got bored with it.

She hands the still unopened bottle back to LYNETTE.

Here. Would you?

LYNETTE *takes the bottle and during the following finishes opening it.* SORREL *rummages in her bag and finds the phone. It is different from the one she used this morning.*

LYNETTE That isn't a new phone, is it?

SORREL No.

LYNETTE Looks different.

SORREL No. *(She answers)* Hallo... Yes? *(She moves to the balcony)* Yes, go on...

She steps outside and closes the door behind her as she listens. LYNETTE *continues with the bottle.*

(in a subdued voice) No, I'm sorry, I don't do that sort of thing. No... No, I'm sorry not even as a special rate, no... Well, if you must know, I think it sounds a bit disgusting, actually, that's why...

A party boat on the river approaches noisily. **SORREL** *sticks a finger in her other ear to hear her caller.* **LYNETTE** *pours two glasses of wine.*

(louder) Disgusting, yes... You heard... Listen, I think you'd better try someone else. Sorry.

LYNETTE *opens the sliding door. She has* **SORREL***'s glass of wine.*

(yelling) No. I'm strictly vanilla. *(Louder)* Vanilla, yes... Bye.

She disconnects.

LYNETTE Here.

SORREL *(startled)* Ah!

LYNETTE What are you doing? Ordering ice cream?

SORREL Just some stupid boy from school. Having a joke.

LYNETTE Which one?

SORREL David Astwick.

LYNETTE Oh, that sweet boy. The one who played Romeo with you?

SORREL That's him.

LYNETTE I was always wanting you to ask him round. You never would.

SORREL No.

LYNETTE I thought he was lovely. A tiny bit spotty perhaps, but...

SORREL He was incredibly spotty. He was all spot.

LYNETTE That's only his age. He'll grow out of it.

SORREL Good. So long as it's not with me.

LYNETTE No wonder you never keep boyfriends. You're so particular.

SORREL Perhaps I've good reason to be, Mother.

Pause. **LYNETTE** *does not rise to this but instead goes into the kitchen where she removes their supper from the microwave.*

LYNETTE *(as she does this)* We've got some left, actually.

SORREL What?

LYNETTE Ice cream. Would you like some? For afters?

SORREL Possibly.

LYNETTE I'll take it out of the freezer, then.

SORREL I'll put these bags away.

LYNETTE Hurry up, it's nearly ready.

SORREL *gathers up the bags and moves to the bedroom with them. As* **SORREL** *is about to go off,* **LYNETTE** *comes back briefly into the living-room.*

Vanilla?

SORREL *(turning, guiltily)* What?

LYNETTE You prefer vanilla?

SORREL Yes, please. Vanilla. Vanilla.

SORREL *goes off.*

LYNETTE *(to herself)* Extraordinary girl. Gets weirder by the day.

As she resumes serving up the meal, the lights fade to blackout.

Scene Three

The same. Early afternoon. A week later.

The room is empty, momentarily.

SORREL *enters. She is in her bathrobe and barefoot, straight from the bath. She is holding two carrier bags. One she sets down by the coffee table, the other she takes to the bar and starts to unpack. It contains some fairly small bottles of a somewhat random selection of alcohol. Whisky, gin, vodka, rum, sweet sherry and tequila.*

The doorbell rings. She freezes. Then runs to the spyhole in the door and looks out.

She opens the door to admit **KELLY**, *who is wearing a smart skirt and blouse and, somewhat incongruously, her old trainers. She is also wearing makeup which serves to make her look slightly more mature. She is holding a fairly bulky package in a chemist's shop bag.*

SORREL Where did you go, you've been ages?

KELLY *(rather breathlessly)* Sorry. I had to wait forever for a bus.

SORREL A bus? Where did you go on a bus?

KELLY To the chemist's.

SORREL There's one just round the corner.

KELLY I know there is. I wasn't going to buy these in there. My mother shops in there. Here.

She hands **SORREL** *the package.*

SORREL What's this?

KELLY You know – thingies.

SORREL I asked for a packet. How many have you bought?

KELLY The girl in the shop said it worked out cheaper in bulk.

SORREL *(examining the box)* There's two hundred in here. What do you think I am?

KELLY She said you soon get through them. She does. Receipt's in the bag.

SORREL I'll pay you back. I'm going to need twelve clients just to finance all this.

KELLY Don't look at me. My building society account is nearly cleaned out. If my mum ever finds out...

SORREL How's she ever going to know?

KELLY She does go through my things occasionally. I know she does. I stick hairs on things and they've moved when I come home.

SORREL That's terrible. She can't do that. Tell her to mind her own business.

KELLY *(sadly)* I couldn't do that. She's my mother.

SORREL Anyway, I said, I'll pay you back. It's the same in any business to start with. You have to invest. God, he'll be here in a minute. I'm not even dressed. Can you help me, please?

KELLY What shall I do?

SORREL Put the magazines out on the table and lay the bar out properly in case he wants a drink and put some sexy music on...

KELLY Right.

SORREL Where are your shoes?

KELLY I took them off. I can't walk in them.

SORREL Well, put them on. You're supposed to be my maid, you look like a PE instructor.

She makes to return to the bedroom.

KELLY Sorrel...

SORREL No.

KELLY What?

SORREL Mandy. You must get used to calling me Mandy.

KELLY Sorry. Mandy...

SORREL And what's your name, again? The name we chose for you?

KELLY *looks blank.*

Oh, for God's sake, Kell! How many more times? Karen.

KELLY Karen. I keep thinking it's Kirstie.

SORREL Would you prefer to be Kirstie?

KELLY No, it's all right. I'll be Karen.

SORREL I don't care if you're Kerry or Caroline, as long as you make up your mind.

KELLY Karen. I'll be Karen.

SORREL Yes, well, remember it. We don't want them knowing our real names, do we?

KELLY *(appalled)* God, no.

SORREL Well, then.

KELLY It's just...Sorrel— *(Hastily)* Sorry, Mandy...

SORREL I have to get ready, Karen. What is it?

KELLY You're certain you want to go through with this, Mandy?

SORREL It's too late now.

KELLY No, it's not too late. When he rings this bell we can tell him he's got the wrong house, that's all. I'll do that if you like.

SORREL We've got this far. We've spent all this money – all your money. We have to go through with it now. We have to.

KELLY I don't mind about the money, I really don't. Forget about the money. I'm worried about you.

SORREL I'll be perfectly fine. I'll probably read a book while I'm doing it.

KELLY But surely, the reason these people – these men – go to people like you, Mandy…is because…there's something possibly wrong with them—

SORREL Not necessarily.

KELLY Then why are they coming to you? Why haven't they got wives or girlfriends?

SORREL I don't know. Maybe they've got unsatisfactory wives or girlfriends, I don't know. Maybe they're not into regular relationships. Maybe they're sad buggers who can't get it at all, like David Astwick. They're not all peculiar. Besides, I've been very careful, haven't I? I haven't taken just anyone, you know. I've been screening my calls extremely carefully. Because yes, you are right. There are some very, very, seriously weird people out there, but I promise you none of them are coming in here.

KELLY In the end you can never be sure, though, can you?

SORREL No more than you would be if you went through a dating agency.

KELLY That's not the same at all.

SORREL Listen, I'm as sure as I can be. I had over forty enquiries initially. You know how picky I've been. I've whittled those right down.

KELLY Yes, to one. I know. But that means, on those figures, for every one normal man there's thirty-nine peculiar ones.

SORREL About average, isn't it?

KELLY Seriously.

SORREL I've got you, haven't I?

KELLY What am I going to do? We get a maniac in here, what am I supposed to do? They're always getting attacked, these women. You read about it all the time. Murdered…and things.

SORREL You only read about the ones that do. I bet lots of them never have any bother at all. Angie never has. Mind you, that's because she beats them up first.

KELLY *(a little tearfully)* I wish you wouldn't make jokes. I'm just so worried about you, Sorrel. Mandy.

SORREL Karen – do not start crying on me, please. That is not helpful. I need you to help me. I'm relying on you. I am not frightened but I am nervous. This is my first client and I want to get it right. I need you, Karen. Yes?

KELLY *stands miserably.*

Kelly?

KELLY Yes. All right.

SORREL I've got to get my stuff on. I may need a hand. Get things ready in here, all right? Come on! It's going to be a piece of piss. Piece of piss! Piece of piss!

SORREL *goes off.*

KELLY *goes behind the bar and cursorily arranges the bottles. She goes to the coffee table and unpacks the carrier bag which* SORREL *has left beside it. It contains some fairly innocuous "girlie" mags.* KELLY *opens one at random.*

KELLY Oh, that's horrible. Urrrgh! Urrrgh!

At arm's length she lays the magazines out on the table.

SORREL *(offstage, in frustration)* Aaaah!

KELLY *(alarmed)* What's wrong?

SORREL *(offstage, urgently)* Karen! Can you come and help me with this thing, please!

KELLY Yes, coming...

KELLY *goes into the bedroom.*

ACT I, SCENE THREE

(offstage, on seeing **SORREL***)* Oh, my God! Sorrel!

SORREL *(offstage)* Can you help me do it up?

The room is empty for a moment. Silence. The doorbell rings.

SORREL *enters, bare-legged in her black basque. She listens.* **KELLY** *comes on behind her, still struggling to finish fastening* **SORREL***'s garment.*

SORREL Are you sure?

KELLY I heard something. *(She struggles)* Stand still!

SORREL Sshh! *(She listens)*

KELLY I'm sure you bought a size too small.

SORREL They're supposed to be tight.

KELLY Not this tight. *(She does it up at last)* There!

SORREL Sshh!

The doorbell rings again.

It was.

KELLY I said it was. *(In panic)* What are we going to do? You're not ready.

SORREL Let him in. I won't be long.

KELLY What do I do with him?

SORREL Entertain him.

KELLY Entertain him? What am I supposed to do, dance on the table?

SORREL Talk to him, just talk to him, Karen.

KELLY I don't think he's come here to talk.

SORREL Well, he'll have to wait, won't he?

KELLY Why do you need to put all that on, anyway?

SORREL It's what they expect. Because they've no imagination of their own, that's why.

KELLY You're only going to take it all off again, aren't you? Presumably.

SORREL I'll have to. I certainly can't do anything with it on. I can't even breathe properly.

KELLY I keep saying, it's too tight. You should have got the bigger size.

The doorbell rings.

SORREL Shut up and answer the door! And put your shoes on! You look ridiculous!

KELLY *moves to the bar to change her shoes.* **SORREL** *starts to go off.* **KELLY** *grabs the box of condoms.*

KELLY Here.

SORREL *(stopping)* What?

KELLY Don't forget these. The thingies.

SORREL You keep them. Make sure you give him some.

KELLY How many?

SORREL I don't know. Two.

KELLY Right.

SORREL No, three – no, make it five. Just in case.

KELLY You're going to make him wear five?

SORREL Not all at once.

The doorbell rings again.

KELLY Five?

SORREL Put on the music. Open the door.

SORREL *goes back into the bedroom.*

> KELLY *replaces the box behind the bar, and slipping off her trainers, climbs into a pair of high-heeled shoes. She totters out, rather unsteadily. She goes to the hi-fi and selects a bland, easy-listening CD. She then steels herself and opens the front door.*
>
> LEO *is standing on the threshold. A dapper man in his forties dressed in a suit. He carriers a small bunch of flowers.*

LEO Ah!

KELLY Hallo.

LEO *(affably)* I was becoming a trifle afraid your doorbell wasn't working.

KELLY No.

LEO It isn't working?

KELLY Yes.

LEO Ah. Splendid.

> *They stand.*
>
> May I come in?

KELLY Yes.

> *She steps well aside to admit* LEO.
>
> LEO *enters the room quite cautiously.* KELLY *closes the front door behind him and watches him apprehensively, ready to take flight at the slightest hint of danger.*

LEO I'm Leo.

KELLY Yes.

LEO And you'll be – Mandy? I take it?

KELLY No.

LEO No? Ah. Then, what's your name?

KELLY Kelly.

LEO Kelly? That's nice.

KELLY No.

LEO It's not nice?

KELLY It's not Kelly.

LEO You're not Kelly?

KELLY No.

Pause.

LEO Who are you, then?

KELLY I'm the maid.

LEO The maid?

KELLY Yes.

LEO Ah. *(He pauses slightly)* Then who's Kelly?

KELLY I don't know.

LEO Ah.

KELLY I've never heard of her.

LEO Oh.

Pause.

What's your name, then?

KELLY's *brain appears to have frozen. She cannot remember the name* **SORREL** *has given her.*

KELLY *(at length)* Kylie.

LEO Oh, that's nice.

Pause.

You're sure about that?

Pause.

Mandy is here, I take it?

KELLY Yes.

LEO Oh, I see. Been a busy day, has it?

KELLY No.

Pause.

LEO *(remembering he is holding the flowers)* These are for her, by the way, just a small token.

KELLY Yes.

LEO Would you like to take them? Do something with them?

He holds out the flowers.

KELLY *(shrinking back)* I'm the maid.

LEO Yes. So you said.

Pause.

I thought you might care to put them in water. The flowers.

KELLY Yes. *(She takes the flowers and stands uncertainly)*

SORREL *(offstage, calling)* Karen!

KELLY *stands frozen.*

Karen!

KELLY *doesn't move.*

LEO Someone appears to be wanting Karen.

KELLY Yes.

SORREL *(offstage, calling)* Karen! Could you come here a second, please?

LEO Who's that wanting Karen?

KELLY Sorrel.

LEO Sorrel? Oh, there's quite a number of you, isn't there? I didn't realize. There's a Sorrel as well?

KELLY No.

LEO Ah.

SORREL *(offstage, calling)* Karen!

LEO Who's Karen?

KELLY Me.

LEO You're Karen?

KELLY Yes.

LEO I thought you were Kylie?

KELLY No.

LEO Then who's Kylie?

KELLY I don't know.

Pause.

Excuse me.

KELLY *totters off abruptly into the bedroom.*

LEO *looks puzzled. He wanders to the coffee table and picks up one of the magazines. He opens one briefly and tuts disapprovingly. He replaces it and goes to the window. The sound of voices from the bedroom.*

SORREL *(offstage, irritably)* Well, offer him something to drink. For God's sake, you can do that, surely, Kelly?

LEO Kelly? Kelly's back, then.

KELLY *enters. She is still holding the flowers.*

LEO Ah! Listen, I was wondering if it would be more convenient if I saw one of the other girls? I mean, if Mandy's busy perhaps I should see someone else?

KELLY Someone else?

LEO I mean Kylie or Sorrel or even Kelly.

KELLY looks at him appalled and goes off again to the bedroom.

LEO looks at his watch and shakes his head.

SORREL *(offstage, angrily)* I'm coming, I'm coming, I'm coming! Get back in there!

LEO Oh.

KELLY comes back, still holding the flowers.

KELLY *(faintly hysterical)* Would you like a drink?

LEO Well, I wouldn't say no to a cup of tea.

KELLY Cup of tea?

This appears to agitate her.

LEO If I may. Is that a problem? Does that present a problem?

KELLY No.

She goes into the kitchen and tries to put the kettle on single-handed. Her other hand is still occupied with holding the flowers. LEO *wanders in after her.*

LEO Can I help at all?

KELLY *(startled)* No.

LEO I'll tell you what, why don't I put those in water for you whilst you're doing that?

KELLY abruptly puts down the flowers and fills the kettle. During the following she puts a tea bag in a mug and waits for the water to boil, all the while keeping a wary eye on LEO.

Now, then. Vase? Vase? Vase? Where do we keep those, I wonder? Any idea where there might be a vase? No? Mind if I have a look?

He looks in a cupboard or two.

SORREL *meanwhile comes out of the bedroom. She now has on the full rig and has done herself up like something from* The Rocky Horror Show. *She makes a slinking entrance entirely for* **LEO**'s *benefit. He, unfortunately, is not there to appreciate it.*

SORREL Hi! I'm Mandy. You must be... Oh. *(She looks round the sitting-room)*

LEO *(going through another cupboard)* There must be one here somewhere, mustn't there?

SORREL, *slightly mystified, goes into the dining area. She sees* **LEO** *scrabbling about under the sink on his hands and knees.*

SORREL Hi! I'm Mandy. You must be... What's going on?

KELLY This is Mandy.

LEO Hallo, Mandy. Be with you in a second, I'm just trying to locate a vase.

SORREL *(rather off-put, to* **KELLY***)* What are you doing with him?

KELLY He's trying to find a vase.

LEO *(emerging with a container)* I think this might do the trick for now. I don't— *(He sees* **SORREL***)* Oh, hallo, you must be Mandy. I'm Leo.

SORREL Hallo, Leo.

LEO I must say that's a very jolly get-up.

SORREL What?

LEO Very festive, for some reason. I don't know why but they always remind me of Christmas, those garments...

SORREL Do they now?

LEO I think it's probably something to do with the panto season. I shudder to think what pantomimes I got taken to as a child but those always tend to remind me of them.

SORREL Great.

KELLY I think you look fantastic.

LEO Oh, she does. Absolute stunner. Absolutely. Is this my tea, thank you very much, Karen. No one else having any? No? Do you mind if I sit down for a moment? Unless anyone's in a desperate hurry.

SORREL Time is money, darling.

LEO Oh, I'm happy to pay, Mandy. I'm more than happy to pay. But I think it would be fair to point out that the clock has only just started running, hasn't it? I mean, delightful as… er, Karen's company has been.

SORREL Well, it's running now.

LEO Absolutely.

They settle in the sitting-room. **SORREL** *chooses the sofa,* **LEO** *the armchair.* **KELLY** *sits as far apart as possible.*

Now, I don't want you to think I do this sort of thing regularly, Mandy. I don't. Not at all. I took a good deep breath before replying to your internet advertisement, I don't mind saying. But in the end, I liked its simplicity, the fact that, unlike some, it didn't try to titivate in a cheap and nasty manner. It was simple and uncluttered, well phrased and most important, if I may say so, in a world where increasingly such things are forgotten or badly taught, extremely well punctuated. I mean, I'm sorry, but I find it impossible to take an advertisement seriously when it is littered with split infinitives and dotted with intrusive apostrophes.

SORREL Well, I'm glad the grammar impressed you.

LEO It did, Mandy, indeed it did. I mean, just because you pursue this line of work doesn't mean that necessarily you have to be semi-literate, does it? That's my stance on that. Anyway, enough of my hobby horses. All I'm saying is, I don't want you to get the wrong idea about me, Mandy. True, I am a widower and, alas, have no significant or long-term relationship at present filling my life. But I am hopeful that all that might, just might, change before long. I can't say any more on that topic as it could compromise a very dear lady friend who does not want the matter circulated just at present. Nonetheless, perhaps I should tell you a little about myself, just to reassure you that my intentions if not perhaps strictly honourable are at the very least harmless. *(He laughs)*

SORREL *looks at her watch pointedly but* LEO *is well away now, apparently oblivious to everything.*

So, very very briefly. My dear late wife, Marjorie, has been departed from us, let's see, just over five years and two months. She was a remarkable and unique woman, Marjorie, and we were an astonishingly closely-knit couple. In fact, I think many people envied us in a lot of ways. Our unity, our contentment, the obvious simple pleasure we took, year in year out, sharing the company of each other. Marriage, you know, is an odd thing, Mandy. I don't know if you've ever been married but people these days often condemn it out of hand, they criticize it, or they treat it with a casualness that takes my breath away sometimes but in the end – in my humble view – if two people are prepared thoroughly to commit to it – to cast aside personal selfishness, self-interest and personal ambition, are willing to love and support each other throughout the vicissitudes and setbacks of modern life, through rough and smooth, thick or thin, sunny or cloudy, uphill or down – it can still be made to work.

SORREL *is now signalling to* KELLY, *who is behind* LEO, *to bring the box of contraceptives. It's quite an elaborate mime but* LEO *still doesn't appear to notice.*

I suppose we were lucky, Marjorie and I. It's quite a fascinating story, actually. We ran this small dry-cleaning business together, you know, which meant we were constantly in each other's pockets, morning, noon and night, all day and every day. But, this is the interesting thing, we never had a moment in which to get bored. That's the secret. We were constantly on the go, always facing up to new challenges. I think therein lies the key. It's very, very interesting this, I inherited the business from my father who in turn had run it in company with my mother for nearly twenty years. That's a piece of history for you, isn't it? How many generations of dry-cleaners can claim that? I tend to think very few indeed. So, I suppose you could say that the—

KELLY *has arrived at* **LEO**'s *elbow with the open box of condoms, which she gently pushes into his field of vision.*

(without really looking) – no, thank you, Karen, I don't want to spoil my supper, just the tea – so I suppose you could, if you like, say the example was there for me to follow.

KELLY *retreats, baffled. She shrugs to* **SORREL**. **SORREL** *now tries another tactic, going through an increasingly elaborate physical display on the sofa, in the vain hope of luring* **LEO** *into her bed.* **LEO** *seems barely to notice this, much to her increasing frustration.*

Marjorie's mother, Ethel, quite apart from being a close personal friend of my mother's, was a valued customer of ours and so it was inevitable, I suppose, that her daughter Marjorie and I would take up with each other. And naturally, as we both grew up, because we lived over the business as we did do for many years – that's another fascinating story, I'll tell you that in a minute – as we lived over the business and Marjorie's parents lived just round the corner, it was perfectly natural that we'd get called in to help out at busy times. Saturday mornings we'd sometimes find ourselves sponging and pressing, even operating some of the machines, but always, of course, under strict supervision. I mean, it was our life, that business. And after I lost Marjorie – following a mercifully short illness – I did consider continuing it. But two years ago my own health took a little turn for the worse – I won't go into that – all under control now – I was urged to sell up and retire. Which I did with some regrets. Unfortunately we were not blessed with children to carry it on so this has, if you like, been the end of an era. In fact, a dynasty, really. But I'll tell you this and this will amaze you, this will. If ever I go back, even today, into a dry-cleaner's – it doesn't matter whose, it doesn't matter where – the moment my nostrils get the whiff of those chemicals – Marjorie's face comes swimming up in front of my eyes. Literally.

SORREL, *owing to her constricted ribcage, is now lying panting on the sofa, exhausted by her abortive sexual display.*

You all right there, Mandy, you seem a trifle uncomfortable? Bit fidgety. If you don't mind my saying, I think you may be wearing that a little bit too tight.

SORREL Really?

LEO You know something really interesting? We always refused to clean those basques. They never dry-clean well, in my experience. It's all the boning in them. Mind you, we did have some extraordinary items pass through our hands in our time. People didn't seem to care. Marjorie used to say, now on what part of her body do you think she wears this? *(He laughs)*

SORREL *gets up, her patience exhausted.*

SORREL I think we need to go in the bedroom now, Leo. I don't think I can contain myself a moment longer.

She grabs his hand and pulls him to his feet.

LEO I haven't quite finished my tea.

SORREL Never mind! This way.

She starts to drag **LEO** *towards the bedroom.*

LEO Well, this is nice. I like a girl with enthusiasm.

KELLY has grabbed a random fistful of condoms, which she presses into LEO's hand.

KELLY Here you are.

LEO Goodness! In for a long session, are we? I'll try and oblige.

SORREL *(pulling him)* This way.

KELLY *(pushing him)* Off you go!

LEO *(as he is borne off)* Now go easy, girls. Remember I'm not as young as I was.

They go off but KELLY rapidly returns and starts to tidy up. She clears the rest of the contraceptives and takes LEO's mug to wash in the sink.

SORREL returns from the bedroom.

SORREL Karen...

KELLY Have you finished already?

SORREL Of course not. He's just getting his clothes off. He wears sock suspenders and a support belt...

KELLY *(in revulsion)* Uurrr!

SORREL I hope he'll be all right. I thought we'd never get him in there. Listen. I think he's safe but you can never tell. Keep an ear out. If I call for help you be in there straightaway with a blunt instrument, all right?

KELLY A blunt instrument?

SORREL Anything. Just to distract him. It'll only be in an emergency. *(She shivers)*

KELLY How do you feel?

SORREL A little bit sick, actually.

KELLY That'll be nerves.

SORREL I don't know what it is. I just feel dreadfully sick all of a sudden. I shouldn't have had that cheeseburger.

A spasm of nausea overcomes her for a moment.

Oh God!

KELLY Well, try not to be sick over him or he might refuse to pay.

SORREL At least we can get everything dry-cleaned cheaply. *(Another spasm)* Oh God!

LEO *(offstage, calling playfully)* Hello-o! Ready when you are, Mandy!

SORREL *gives a little nervous squeak of apprehension.*

KELLY *(grasping* SORREL*'s hands briefly)* Good luck!

SORREL Yes.

SORREL *goes into the bedroom.*

KELLY *is very nervous for her friend. She paces about, listening out. In a moment,* SORREL*'s sexual noises start up. She is frankly not the greatest faker of orgasms. Her moans and sighs are more reminiscent of Lear than Leander. As the sounds grow increasingly desperate,* KELLY *becomes more alarmed. She hunts round for a weapon. In the end she selects the temporary vase, removing the flowers to the sink and emptying the water from it. She clutches it like a weapon.* SORREL*'s cries become quite passionate.* KELLY *takes a sudden unilateral decision and, kicking off her shoes, races into the bedroom with the vase.*

SORREL *(offstage, passionately)* Ah! Ah! Ah! Ah!

LEO *(offstage, in pain)* Ow!

SORREL *(offstage)* What are you doing?

KELLY *(offstage)* I came to help you.

LEO *(offstage)* Why'd you do that?

SORREL *(offstage)* You idiot!

KELLY *(offstage)* Sorry.

LEO *(offstage)* What'd she do that for?

SORREL *(offstage)* Sorry, Leo. Excuse us a minute, will you?

LEO *(offstage)* I need to lie down now.

SORREL *(offstage)* I'll be back in a minute.

> **SORREL** *enters with* **KELLY,** **SORREL** *pulling on her bathrobe.*
>
> *(fiercely)* You stupid idiot.

KELLY *(upset)* I didn't know, did I?

SORREL You could have killed him.

KELLY I only hit him on the shoulder.

SORREL Yes. It was the shock, though. You could have killed us both, come to that.

KELLY I thought you were in trouble. You were making those terrible noises...

SORREL Those were...sexual noises. That's all. Can't you tell the difference?

KELLY Didn't sound like it to me. Do you always make that noise?

SORREL No. Not usually, not like that...only...with this you're expected to make some noise, aren't you?

KELLY You are? Why?

SORREL It makes them feel they're doing it right, that's all.

KELLY Oh.

SORREL I'd better get back. Finish off.

KELLY How are you feeling?

SORREL Dreadful. Really dreadful.

KELLY Can't you stop?

SORREL I can't stop now. We're only halfway.

KELLY *(miserably)* Oh.

SORREL *(turning as she goes)* Kell.

KELLY Mmm!

SORREL Turn the music up. Then you don't have to listen.

KELLY You sure?

SORREL I'll be fine, don't worry.

KELLY *(gratefully)* Thank you.

> SORREL *exits to the bedroom.*

> KELLY *crosses to the CD player and turns up the volume. The easy-listening bland music fills the room. Next door,* SORREL *starts up again.*

SORREL *(in feigned ecstasy)* Ah! Ah! Ah! Ah!

> KELLY *turns the music even louder to drown* SORREL *out. She starts singing somewhat tunelessly along with the music, anything to shut out the bedroom sounds.*

> SORREL *enters from the bedroom in a state of shock.*

> *She stands swaying in the doorway. She clutches her robe around her, protectively.* KELLY *at last sees her. She hastily switches off the music.*

KELLY Sorrel? Sorrel?

> SORREL *seems to be having trouble breathing.*

What's wrong?

SORREL *(sitting, speaking with difficulty)* I don't think I can do this, Kell. I don't think I can do this.

> *She starts to pant now, rather as if she was going into labour.*

I can't do it. I can't do it...

As her panic attack continues, **KELLY** *holds her, comforting her.*

KELLY *(sadly)* I don't know why you ever thought you could.

A moment and **LEO** *returns, fully dressed.*

LEO *(brightly)* Thank you very much indeed. Most enjoyable. I've left the money on your dressing table, Mandy. That's in order. It's all there. But if you want to count it I shan't be in the least... (He sees* **SORREL**'s *condition)* She all right, is she?

KELLY Yes, she's just...she's just feeling a little bit—

LEO Ah, well. Probably the excitement. I must say I feel a little— Hah!

Quite suddenly, he appears to have been struck a massive blow by an invisible sledgehammer. He falls to his knees, evidently in great pain. In great surprise.

Oh!

He looks at them.

Oh!

With a last look around the room and indeed the world.

Oh!

He falls on his face and lies still.

The women stare at him. **SORREL** *is quiet now. Tentatively,* **KELLY** *goes over to* **LEO** *and cautiously examines him.*

KELLY *(in a whisper)* Sorrel, he's not breathing. He's dead. He's dead. He's dead.

SORREL *(softly)* Oh, God.

Blackout.

Curtain.

ACT II

Scene One

The same. Later that evening, around 11 p.m.

SORREL sits at the desk. She is staring at the screen of her laptop. But her mind seems on other things. She is in her bathrobe, without make-up and looks very pale and unhappy.

LYNETTE comes from the bedroom. She is in her dressing gown, ready for bed. She looks at SORREL anxiously.

LYNETTE I wish you'd go to bed, Sorrel.

SORREL *(muted)* I don't want to go to bed.

LYNETTE You look terrible. If you're not better in the morning, I'm dragging you to the doctor's. Whether you like it or not.

SORREL There's nothing wrong, I've said.

LYNETTE You haven't eaten a thing. You've had no supper at all.

SORREL I didn't want anything.

LYNETTE You're not going anorexic on me as well, are you?

SORREL Do I look anorexic?

LYNETTE You can't always tell.

Silence.

What happened today?

SORREL What do you mean?

LYNETTE You were perfectly fine this morning. When I left. I come home and find you like this.

SORREL Things change. I'm a teenager. I get mood swings. Sorry.

LYNETTE Something happened.

SORREL Nothing happened.

LYNETTE I know when you're lying.

SORREL *(angrily)* Will you just leave me alone, please?

LYNETTE All right.

She coughs. She goes to her bag and with great deliberation takes out a cigarette and lights it. She sits in the armchair.

SORREL *watches her for a moment.* **LYNETTE** *stares back.*

SORREL *(at length)* Why are you doing that?

LYNETTE To annoy you.

SORREL I see.

LYNETTE If you're going to shout at me, be thoroughly objectionable for no reason at all, I thought I'd better give you a reason.

SORREL Talk about me being childish.

LYNETTE Well, we're all children underneath, Sorrel. Didn't you know that? We appear to grow older – visibly anyway – our faces sag, our boobs droop, our bums drop, but the irony is that inside we still feel the same as we always did. It's other people that change us. Start to treat us differently. The young ones, the ones that used to be our contemporaries but no longer are, they grow wary of us, mistrust us with their secrets, shut us out. Because after all, what could we possibly understand any more. And that's just the girls. As for the young men, the ones you used to have panting for you on the end of a lead. They don't even notice you exist.

SORREL Rubbish.

LYNETTE They don't, most of them look straight through you. Unless, for some reason, you remind them of their mother. They pass me in the street, I could be a bloody litter bin as far as they're concerned. Except at least then I'd be some use. You know I went to this party, a couple of years ago. Some colleague, same age as me – Richard Turnbull, I think it was – he was having his fortieth party, just a few friends. And I turned up a bit late and when I got there, I thought, oh God, he's invited all these old *elderly* people. Why has he done this? Am I the only young one here? And then suddenly I realized, of course, I wasn't. I was just another boring old elderly person.

SORREL What's the matter with you tonight?

LYNETTE You're asking me? I'm allowed to be a moody teenager too, you know. Just because I'm forty-two, it doesn't mean I can't be a teenager.

SORREL Forty-two is not old.

LYNETTE Don't you believe it. It's bloody old.

Pause.

The point is, I can't do this all alone, Sorrel. I need you. If you shut me out, I can't cope. I'll just fall to pieces. I'm sorry. I know mothers are supposed to do better than that but I'm afraid I'm not that good.

SORREL *gets up and moves to the sofa.*

SORREL Come on, give us one of those.

LYNETTE What?

SORREL A cigarette.

LYNETTE I don't believe it.

SORREL Come on.

LYNETTE You don't want a cigarette.

SORREL Yes, I do.

LYNETTE No, you don't, they're bad for you.

SORREL Nonsense. Where'd you read that?

LYNETTE You really want one?

SORREL I just said.

LYNETTE Just one, then.

She gives **SORREL** *a cigarette. She lights it for her.*

I hope you're not going to start smoking.

SORREL Well, I was hoping it might cure my anorexia.

LYNETTE We can't afford it. Not both of us. We can only subsidize one of us.

SORREL Tell you what, why don't we both make a vow that this is our last cigarette. Then tomorrow we can both give up together. How about that?

LYNETTE There's a flaw in that logic somewhere.

She stubs out her cigarette.

I must go to bed.

Suddenly weary.

I've taken a pill, I must give it a chance to work.

SORREL Drug addict as well.

LYNETTE That's me.

She goes to the bedroom door.

God, some nights I miss him so much, you know.

SORREL Dad? You can't do. How can you? How can you miss that man?

LYNETTE I know to you that sounds so absurd. And I don't want to sound elderly, but one day you'll understand. You can't choose to love someone, Sorrel. Or to stop loving them sometimes. I wish it was that simple. I really do. 'Night.

SORREL 'Night. Sleep well.

LYNETTE *goes off to the bedroom.*

(softly) I hope.

She takes a final drag on her cigarette and coughs.

These are disgusting. How can she do it?

She stubs out her cigarette and goes to her bag. She takes out her everyday mobile and speed-dials a number.

(Into the phone) Hi! Give it half an hour, then come down… she's taken a pill, she's in bed…yes, it's high tide at the moment, so it needs to be soon… There's nothing, don't panic. The first thing I did was take us off the website. There's no way to trace us… Listen, just wait outside, I'll let you in. *(Fiercely)* And Kell! Will you please stop panicking!

She disconnects and starts switching off and closing up her laptop.

In her bag, her other mobile rings. She hesitates but as it continues to ring she looks nervously towards the bedroom. She reaches in her bag and answers it.

Hallo. No, I'm afraid Mandy is no longer available, I'm sorry. No, this is her mother speaking. Goodbye.

She disconnects and switches off the phone with a certain finality. She smiles rather ruefully, then gathers up her bag and her laptop.

SORREL *goes off to the bedroom. As she goes she switches off the lights at the door.*

In the darkness outside, a party boat passes, as rowdy as ever. Its lights reflect briefly into the room then fade with the receding sound.

A pause. Time has passed.

ACT II, SCENE ONE

In the darkness, **SORREL** *creeps in from the bedroom. She has on her tracksuit now.*

She creeps towards the front door. She opens it carefully. The following scene is played as quietly as possible.

(in a whisper) Quickly, come in.

KELLY *slips in through the door. She is also in her tracksuit but in addition wears her woollen gloves and a ski-mask.*

What the hell are you wearing?

KELLY My ski-mask.

SORREL What's the point of that?

KELLY So I won't be recognized.

SORREL He's hardly going to recognize you, is he? He's been dead for ten hours.

KELLY Your mother might see me.

SORREL If my mother catches us, we're dead. Take it off.

KELLY *reluctantly removes the mask.*

Follow me.

KELLY Where is he?

SORREL Still under my bed.

KELLY God! How could you sleep…?

SORREL Sleep…!

KELLY …with him lying underneath you like that?

SORREL Do you honestly think I've had any sleep? With a dead body in my room? I had to undress him, that was bad enough.

KELLY *(in horror)* Undress him?

SORREL I'll get rid of his clothes later. It'll be more difficult to identify him, that way.

KELLY What are you going to do with them?

SORREL Don't worry, I'll think of something. Ready, then?

KELLY I suppose. Are his eyes still open?

SORREL I couldn't close them for some reason. They kept opening again.

KELLY Oh, dear God...this is so wrong...so wrong...

SORREL It is not wrong. It's the only way. Listen, I've wrapped him in a blanket, you won't see much, I promise.

KELLY This is so wrong, we'll go to hell, I know we will.

SORREL Don't worry, we're already there. Come on.

They both sneak into the bedroom. A moment later they return, dragging something heavy in a blanket.

Ssshh! Quietly.

KELLY He's so heavy.

SORREL Ssshh! My mother's just along there.

KELLY *(tearfully)* He was such a nice man.

SORREL He was not a nice man at all, Kelly. He was a very boring little hypocrite who gave lectures about marriage and went to prostitutes.

KELLY You can't say that about him. Not now.

SORREL It's not going to bother him, is it?

KELLY Should we say a few words? Before we tip him over?

SORREL Oh, for God's sake, Kell. Come on, pull, girl.

KELLY It's difficult to get a proper grip.

SORREL Then take those stupid gloves off. Why are you wearing gloves, anyway?

KELLY I don't want to leave fingerprints.

SORREL Kelly, I hate to tell you, but this flat is littered with your fingerprints. What the hell difference is it going to make?

KELLY I might leave some on him.

SORREL You can't leave fingerprints on dead bodies.

KELLY You never know, not these days. They can trace you through anything. Hairs, bits of dead skin...

SORREL Then why are you bothering with gloves?

They pause for breath at the windows.

Right. The tide's still up. Now, this is the only risky bit. As soon as I open the windows, we get him over the rail as quick as we can. But don't let the blanket go. That's the only thing that can link us to him. OK?

KELLY OK.

SORREL I'll check the coast is clear.

She cautiously slides open the window a little and sticks her nose out.

KELLY *(singing softly, meanwhile)* I DANCED IN THE MORNING
WHEN THE WORLD WAS BEGUN,
AND I DANCED IN THE MOON
AND THE STARS AND THE SUN—

SORREL What are you up to now?

KELLY Just something to...see him off...

SORREL Well, keep it down. Come on, it's all clear!

During the following, they heave the body out on to the balcony and, with difficulty, prop it against the rail.

KELLY
AND I CAME DOWN FROM HEAVEN
AND I DANCED ON THE EARTH,
AT BETHLEHEM I HAD MY BIRTH.

DANCE, THEN, WHEREVER YOU MAY BE,
I AM THE LORD OF THE DANCE, SAID HE—

SORREL That's it! OK. Heave!

As they heave the body over, **SORREL** *joins* **KELLY** *in the last two lines.*

KELLY AND SORREL
AND I'LL LEAD YOU ALL, WHEREVER YOU MAY BE,
AND I'LL LEAD YOU ALL IN THE DANCE, SAID HE.

Hup!

The body hits the water with a splash. They both lean against the rail, catching their breath.

LYNETTE *comes blearily out of the bedroom. She has on her dressing gown. She sees* **SORREL** *and* **KELLY** *on the balcony.*

LYNETTE What are you two doing?

SORREL Oh. Hallo, Mum.

KELLY Hallo, Mrs Saxon.

LYNETTE What are you doing here, Kelly? It's the middle of the night.

KELLY It was such a beautiful evening and I phoned Sorrel and asked if I could stand on your balcony for a minute, Mrs Saxon…

LYNETTE What are you talking about? It's a terrible night. It's freezing cold, there isn't even a moon. Now come in at once, both of you.

SORREL *and* **KELLY** *traipse in.*

(with an awful thought) You weren't out there smoking drugs or something, were you? Please tell me you weren't out there doing something you shouldn't have been?

SORREL No, we were just…singing, that's all. *(She giggles)*

LYNETTE Singing?

KELLY *(also finding it funny)* We were singing.

SORREL Singing...

Both of them go into a fit of girlish giggling. They are both clearly out of control. **LYNETTE** *stares at them in horror.*

LYNETTE Oh, no. You're both on drugs, I know you are.

She continues to watch them.

They roll about helplessly out of control, as the lights fade to blackout.

Scene Two

The same. A fortnight later. Late afternoon.

The room is in darkness. It is now a week before Christmas. A small decorated tree stands by the window. A few cards are dotted about.

In a moment, **SORREL** *enters and switches on the lights at the front door. She is just home from school and is dressed accordingly. She has her usual backpack and wears a coat, scarf and hat. She is currently talking on her mobile.*

SORREL *(entering)* ...no...no, he didn't... I don't care...no, if he wants to go out with you, he has to ask you himself...yes...

She closes the door, dumps her bag and starts removing her hat and coat.

...no, Kell, that is not the point at all...you let him treat you like a – like a toilet...well, he is...he's using you whenever it suits him...whenever he gets the urge...yes, well...don't let him...hold out, girl...he'll be back... Listen, you want to go out tonight? Movie maybe. Yes? I dunno, I'll look. There's a good one on at the— Hallo? Kell, hallo? Are you still there?

She stares at her phone. The batteries are dead. She growls at it.

Oh.

She reaches into her pack and exchanges her phone for the other one. She switches it on, studies the display and is evidently delighted with what she sees. She keys in the number and listens. During the following she sits at the desk.

Sorry about that. No, dead battery. Listen – no, I'm on the other one. Yes, we were saying. Well, come down later and let's decide then…or a pizza, yes… Yes, OK… Hey, Kell, incidentally I just switched this phone on – I haven't turned it on for days…no, I was going to get rid of it eventually…but there've been no more messages…no, it's over, Kell. We did it. It's all right…it's been two weeks, now…more than that… we're safe…no, if they were going to…no, if they were…Kell, no one will ever know. All right. Trust me. I'm your friend.

The sound of a key in the front door.

Kell, I can't talk any more… I have to go now. See you later.

She ends the call and slips the phone into the desk drawer. She starts casually looking at a Christmas card.

LYNETTE *enters. She is in good spirits. She carries a carrier bag.*

Hi, Mum.

LYNETTE Hallo, darling. Have a good day?

SORREL Pretty good.

LYNETTE Well, you're not going to believe my day.

She kisses her.

SORREL Why?

LYNETTE You wait till I tell you.

She reaches into the carrier and waves a bottle of pink champagne. A small vocal fanfare.

Tarra-tum-tarra-tum-tarrra-tum.

SORREL What's that?

LYNETTE Pink champagne.

SORREL Why?

LYNETTE I got a job!

SORREL You did?

LYNETTE A real proper job.

She holds out her arms. They embrace excitedly.

SORREL *(overjoyed for her)* How did you do that? I mean, you never said anything. I never knew you were...

LYNETTE I didn't want to tell you before. I didn't want to tell you in case it didn't work out. There've been so many false alarms...

SORREL Yes, but when?

LYNETTE I had the interview this lunchtime. I had the preliminary last week and then he asked me back and offered it to me on the spot. Just like that. I nearly phoned you and then I thought, no, I want to tell you in person... Oh, darling, it's a wonderful job... I mean, it's not the most brilliant money – but the prospects are terrific... I just know I can make it work for us...

SORREL I'm so happy for you. You must tell me everything... all about it...

LYNETTE I will. I'll just put this in the fridge. Hang on. I got us a special meal as well. I went in Selfridges' Food Hall and went completely mad. Spent a fortune and I don't care.

SORREL What's the job, though?

LYNETTE Well, you're not to laugh at this... It's this religious publishers...

SORREL Religious?

LYNETTE Well, you know, they publish a lot of Christian material. They're American-based originally and they're just getting going over here – you know, specialist books... Penny told me about it – you remember Penny Trent – short blonde woman – rather red-faced...

SORREL Oh yes, vaguely.

LYNETTE Anyway, she tipped me off about it – because in her job she deals with this firm all the time – and she'd heard on the grapevine that they were anxious to develop the internet side of the business in Europe – and she thought it would be tailor-made for me, which of course it is – so I met them last Thursday and they seemed keen then but they said, look, come back next week – like today – because they had two other candidates and I thought, God, here we go again – and this morning I got there and I'd barely sat down and they said, it's yours if you want it and when can you start? And I said, how about yesterday—?

Her volubility has brought on a bout of coughing. She goes for a cigarette.

And I'm seriously going to give up, I promise. Look, I'll show you what I bought for dinner...

SORREL Mum, would it be all right if I invited Kelly to eat with us?

LYNETTE *(rather coolly)* Kelly? I suppose so. I'd have thought you'd see enough of her during the day. I was rather hoping it could just be the two of us for once. Still, ask her down, if you want to.

SORREL It's just I'd arranged to go out with her tonight and she's going through a bit of a *crise* and I—

LYNETTE No, well then, go out if you'd prefer...

SORREL No, I want to stay here with you.

LYNETTE If you've already arranged something—?

SORREL I haven't arranged anything...

LYNETTE Well, you obviously have, otherwise you wouldn't—

SORREL *(slightly irritably)* Listen, I want to stay home with you. I want to celebrate with you—

LYNETTE Well, you don't have to stay in if you don't want to—

SORREL *(yelling)* I want to.

Silence.

(softly) God!

LYNETTE I don't know why you suddenly need to shout.

SORREL Because everything becomes a great saga.

Silence.

LYNETTE You go out if you'd prefer to.

SORREL *(sharply)* Don't start again!

A long silence.

LYNETTE You always manage to ruin everything, don't you?

Silence. **SORREL** *breathes deeply, asserting great self-control.*

I mean, I never ask you for much, do I? I think compared with other mothers I'm extremely reasonable.

Silence. **SORREL** *grinds her teeth.*

I ask for one tiny little celebration with just the two of us and you manage to spoil even that.

She sniffs. Her eyes are filling with tears.

I was so excited on the way home. I thought you'd be so thrilled.

SORREL I am thrilled.

LYNETTE I thought you'd be so happy for me.

SORREL I said I was.

LYNETTE Born selfish. It's always about you, isn't it? It has to be about you, the whole time. You're just like your father—

SORREL Right. That's it. That is it. I'm sorry, I am out of here.

LYNETTE That's right. Off you go.

SORREL Start comparing me to that bastard—

LYNETTE I'll be fine. Don't worry. I'll have the champagne on my own.

SORREL You do that. *(Opening the front door)* I hope it chokes you, you stupid bi—

DAN and GRACE are standing there, apparently just about to ring the bell. DAN is a fairly stocky man in his forties. GRACE, rather severe, in her thirties.

(startled) Oh.

DAN Good evening.

SORREL Evening.

DAN *(holding up his ID)* Detective Sergeant Endicott. This is WPC Page. I wonder if we could have a few words.

SORREL *(faintly)* A few words?

DAN Just a few. Your mum at home, is she?

LYNETTE *(from the kitchen)* Who is it?

GRACE Your dad home, is he, love?

SORREL No, my father's – he's not here.

LYNETTE *(from the kitchen)* Sorrel, who are you talking to?

SORREL It's the police.

LYNETTE The what?

She comes out of the kitchen and sees them.

Oh. What do you...?

DAN Good evening, madam. May we come in for a minute?

LYNETTE *(bewildered)* Yes, I suppose so.

DAN and GRACE step past SORREL and into the flat, closing the door.

Has something happened? I mean, has there been an accident?

DAN In a manner of speaking...

LYNETTE Someone we know?

DAN It's possible.

LYNETTE Is it my husband? Has something happened...?

DAN Shall we sit down for a minute?

GRACE As far as we know nothing's happened to your husband, Mrs Saxon.

LYNETTE How did you know I was Mrs—?

DAN Should we sit down, would that be a good idea?

LYNETTE No, I'd like to know why you're here before I—

GRACE I don't think we need the youngster here, do we, sergeant?

DAN No, we won't need her.

GRACE Got somewhere you were going, were you, love? Somewhere you'd like to go and play?

SORREL Go and *what*?

DAN Just while we talk to your mum, love. We just want to ask her a few questions, we won't be long.

SORREL What do you want with my mother?

GRACE Off you go, love.

SORREL No, I'm staying here. I want to know what you want with my mother.

LYNETTE Sorrel, you'd better do as they say.

SORREL No, I'm sorry. I'm not leaving here.

DAN *(still perfectly reasonably)* Listen, love, we can do this in two ways. We can have a quiet chat with your mum alone here. Or we can ask her to come down to the police station and talk to her there. Which do you prefer?

Pause.

SORREL I'll be in my room, Mum. If you want me. You just call.

DAN That's a good girl.

> **SORREL** *glares at him and goes off to the bedroom.*

Fine young lady. You must be very proud of her.

LYNETTE Yes, I am.

DAN Now. Shall we sit down?

> **DAN** *and* **LYNETTE** *sit facing each other.* **GRACE** *wanders around the room in a rather predatory manner.* **DAN** *takes out a notebook.*

LYNETTE Well?

DAN Yes, well, we'll make this as quick as we can. I'm sure you've got lots to get on with at this busy time of year. Just as we have. We're investigating a death which we've reason to believe may have occurred under suspicious circumstances.

LYNETTE Who?

DAN Er...the victim's name is Leo Graham Tyler.

LYNETTE Tyler?

DAN Correct.

LYNETTE Never heard of him.

GRACE You'd probably have known him just as Leo, dear.

LYNETTE Would I?

DAN You know anyone called Leo?

LYNETTE No. I don't know any Leos at all.

DAN Sure about that?

LYNETTE Positive.

> *Pause.*

GRACE He could have used a false name.

DAN Possibly.

He produces a photograph.

LYNETTE What is this?

DAN *(handing it to her)* That face ring a bell at all?

LYNETTE *(studying the photo)* No.

GRACE No?

LYNETTE Don't know him at all. Who is he?

DAN Want to have another quick look? Make sure?

LYNETTE No, I don't want another quick look. I want to know what this is about?

DAN You go out to work at all, Mrs Saxon?

LYNETTE Yes, I do.

DAN What line would that be?

LYNETTE I'm...well, I'm between jobs just at present...I'm starting a new one next week. I'm a...an internet consultant.

DAN Ah. The internet. That's the thing, isn't it, these days?

LYNETTE Certainly is.

DAN They say you can buy just about anything on the internet, these days, don't they?

LYNETTE True.

DAN They say there's nothing you can't buy. So that's what you're doing at the moment, is it? Internet consultant. And who's consulting you just at present?

LYNETTE As I say, I'm currently between jobs at present. I'm doing some...office cleaning just to fill in.

DAN Office cleaning?

LYNETTE Yes.

DAN Enjoy that, do you?

LYNETTE It's all right.

GRACE Do you do a lot of scrubbing, do you?

LYNETTE I'm sorry?

GRACE Do you find yourself doing a lot of scrubbing?

DAN That'll do, Grace.

LYNETTE What on earth are you talking about?

DAN So we've established, then, that you have never met or heard of Mr Tyler and that you are working currently as an office cleaner. We correct on that score, are we?

LYNETTE Perfectly correct. Was that all you wanted to know, because I have supper to make?

GRACE What about Mandy? Does the name Mandy mean anything to you?

LYNETTE Mandy? No, I don't know anyone called Mandy.

DAN What would your own name be, may I ask?

LYNETTE My name is Lynette.

GRACE No, that doesn't sound a lot like Mandy, does it?

DAN Can't say it does.

GRACE Unless she's using a false name as well.

DAN Mandy, you mean?

GRACE Absolutely. "For the lips of a strange woman drop as an honeycomb, and her mouth is smoother than oil."

LYNETTE What?

DAN You'll have to pardon my colleague, Mrs Saxon. Grace is given to biblical quotations when the occasion arises...

GRACE "But her end is bitter as wormwood, sharp as a two-edged sword."

LYNETTE Are you the police or Jehovah's Witnesses?

DAN Ah, you know, I think we occasionally overlap on that. Certainly do working with WPC Page, there. We have a saying at the station – if Grace can't arrest them, she converts them.

He smiles.

LYNETTE *(unamused)* Is that it, then?

GRACE Mr Tyler was dragged out of the river a little over a week ago. A mile downstream of here. Just beyond Greenwich. They were able to calculate from the estimated speed of the tide and from the approximate period the body had been in the water that it had probably fallen in or had been pushed in, or had been dropped in, somewhere not far from here.

LYNETTE How tragic. Who was this man, anyway?

DAN Mr. Tyler was retired. He'd taken early retirement to enjoy his middle years. Apparently he was formerly the owner of a dry-cleaning business.

LYNETTE Rather unfortunate. A dry-cleaner getting drowned, isn't it?

She laughs a little nervously.

DAN I'm sure his family would find that highly amusing.

LYNETTE Sorry.

GRACE "Even in laughter the heart is sorrowful."

DAN There you are. You've set her off again, now, with another burst of Deuteronomy.

GRACE Proverbs.

DAN Proverbs. Beg your pardon, Grace.

LYNETTE Well, I'm very sorry he was drowned, of course I am, but—

She has a small coughing fit and fumbles automatically for a cigarette.

DAN *(solicitously)* All right?

ACT II, SCENE TWO

LYNETTE Yes, thank you. Sorry, would you...?

She proffers the cigarettes. **GRACE** *shakes her head.*

DAN No, thank you. No, the problem is, you see, Lynette – may I call you Lynette? – the problem is, he was taken out of the water but it appears he wasn't drowned – he died of a heart attack some hours earlier. Which leads us to believe that he must have been placed in the water subsequently.

LYNETTE Unless he died whilst balancing precariously on a bridge.

DAN *(staring at* **LYNETTE***)* I don't think she's taking this seriously, Grace, do you?

GRACE It doesn't appear to me she is, Dan.

DAN *(more briskly)* Answer me this, then, Lynette. Do you advertise on the internet at all, do you?

LYNETTE Advertise? What would I advertise?

DAN You set yourself up as an internet consultant, I thought you might advertise on it.

LYNETTE Well, I don't.

GRACE Never?

LYNETTE Never.

DAN So you've never advertised so-called personal services using the name – I quote – "Randy Mandy" on a web site known as Lovechicks dot co dot uk?

LYNETTE My God! Certainly not.

DAN So it would surprise you to know, would it, that Leo Tyler made regular use of the services of Lovechicks dot co dot uk and that it was listed on his PC as being among his personal favourites?

LYNETTE How sad.

GRACE You own a mobile phone, do you?

LYNETTE Yes.

DAN Got it with you at present, by any chance?

LYNETTE Yes, I have.

GRACE Know the number offhand?

LYNETTE Yes, of course I do.

DAN Would you mind giving it to me, please?

LYNETTE Why should I?

GRACE Because that way, you will be assisting us with our enquiries.

DAN But if you don't give it to us, equally you could be accused of trying to obstruct the course of justice.

GRACE "The heart is deceitful above all things, and desperately wicked."

DAN She said it. Not me.

LYNETTE 0783 561610.

DAN *(writing this down)* Six—one—six—one—zero. Is it switched on at present?

LYNETTE Yes. I'm sure it is.

GRACE Where is it?

LYNETTE In my bag, do you want me to…?

DAN No, leave it there. That's all right. So if I phone this number now, the chances are that phone of yours will ring?

LYNETTE Chances are.

GRACE If it's the right number.

LYNETTE It is.

DAN OK, then. Shall we give it a go. See what happens?

LYNETTE Be my guest.

ACT II, SCENE TWO 73

DAN *produces his own mobile and starts to punch up the number which* LYNETTE *has given him.*

DAN *(keying in the number)* Zero—seven—eight... Here we go. Miracles of science.

He completes the number and sends.

A silence. From her bag, LYNETTE*'s phone rings.*

Well, that certainly works, anyway.

LYNETTE Wonderful things, mobile phones.

DAN Aren't they just? To think it was only a few years ago, we'd hardly heard of them. Now we can't manage without them, can we?

LYNETTE True.

DAN Kids especially.

LYNETTE Yes.

DAN You'd think their ear was superglued to it, some of them.

LYNETTE Absolutely.

Pause.

DAN *(shaking his head)* I don't know.

Pause.

LYNETTE That it then? Can I—

GRACE Do you own a second phone by any chance?

LYNETTE What?

GRACE A second mobile phone?

DAN Oh, that's good thinking, Grace, I hadn't thought of that.

LYNETTE No, I don't.

GRACE So if we were to ring the number provided by Randy Mandy at Lovechicks dot co dot uk, nothing else is likely to ring in your bag, is it?

LYNETTE No way.

GRACE Worth a go, though, isn't it?

DAN Oh, yes, certainly worth a go.

LYNETTE *(still mildly amused)* Just as you like.

DAN I've still got that number somewhere, haven't I, Grace? I don't think I threw it— *(He finds a scrap of paper)* No, here we are. I know I wrote it down. In case I got lonely over Christmas.

He punches in the number.

GRACE *(disapprovingly)* "Lust not after her beauty in thine heart; neither let her take thee with her eyelids..."

DAN Only joking, Grace, only joking. There we are. Now. Do we hear anything or don't we?

They listen, staring at the bag. From the desk drawer, SORREL's *mobile starts to ring.*

Oh, we do.

GRACE *takes* SORREL's *phone from the drawer and puts it on the desk top.*

LYNETTE *(the whole picture clear)* Oh, my God.

DAN Call you Mandy now, can I?

GRACE *(murmuring contemptuously)* "As a jewel of gold in a swine's snout..."

SORREL *appears in the bedroom doorway.*

They all look at her.

SORREL Mum...?

DAN We haven't quite finished yet, love...

SORREL What's happening?

LYNETTE Go back in there, please, Sorrel.

SORREL I just heard my phone ring, I thought...

LYNETTE No, that was my phone ringing. Not yours.

SORREL No, it was definitely...

LYNETTE No, your phone is still in your bag here, I know it is. That was my phone.

SORREL But that—

LYNETTE (*firmly*) It was my phone.

Silence.

DAN How many phones have you got, you two?

LYNETTE I have two. She has one.

DAN I see. One for business.

GRACE One for pleasure.

LYNETTE Quite correct.

DAN So you're denying none of this?

LYNETTE I...I admit some of it. I know absolutely nothing about— (*She glances at* SORREL) ...about what happened to that man.

DAN You want to go back in the bedroom for a minute, love?

SORREL No, I don't.

DAN Now, I'm telling you, you go in your room at once.

LYNETTE Don't tell her what to do.

DAN Go back to your room.

LYNETTE (*angrily*) Don't you dare start ordering my daughter about, you—

DAN (*suddenly very violently*) Listen, Mandy, you can stop all that right now. All right? You may have a posh voice and a smart flat but as far as we're concerned you're just another second-rate tom who opens her legs and uses it as a money box, so don't come the stuck-up bitch with me, right? Now, we've been very pleasant with you up till now, very, very civil indeed. You've been lying to us through your crooked little teeth since the minute we walked in here and we have been patient with you, we've been restrained and understanding because of your kiddy here. But enough is enough, sweetheart. Now either you tell us what happened between you and this Leo Tyler or I'll have Grace here handcuff you, frogmarch you down the station, bang you up in a cell and throw away the bloody key, all right?

LYNETTE *is quite shaken by this. Silence.*

SORREL (*quietly*) This has nothing to do with my mother.

DAN What? You still here? I told you to go back to your room.

SORREL This has nothing to do with her. That is my phone. She knows nothing about all—

DAN Grace, will you escort the young lady back to her room, please?

GRACE (*moving towards* **SORREL**) Come on, come with me, love.

SORREL You touch me, I shall sue you for harassment and police brutality. This whole thing is my idea. I set it up on the internet, nobody else was involved. My mother did not know about it. Mandy was me. I did it all. I invited Leo round here. I did it to earn money. Only he suddenly died. Accidentally. And I had to get rid of him. That's all. It was me.

They stare at her.

LYNETTE She's talking nonsense.

DAN You dragged his body out of the bedroom, then, did you?

SORREL Yes.

DAN Out on to that balcony there, did you?

SORREL Right.

DAN And then – what – you just tossed it over the rail?

SORREL Yes. With difficulty.

DAN And you did that all on your own, did you? You say no one else was involved?

SORREL does not reply.

Eh? Anyone else?

SORREL *(quietly)* No one.

GRACE What did you do with his clothes?

SORREL What?

GRACE How did you dispose of them?

SORREL I took them to a charity shop.

DAN Which one?

SORREL British Heart Foundation.

Pause.

DAN Well, it's sort of fitting, anyway.

GRACE We could check.

DAN *(shaking his head)* No point. Even if she's telling the truth, some social worker's probably wearing them by now. *(To* **SORREL***)* Listen, come here. Come on. Come over here. I'm not going to bite you. That's it. Sit here.

SORREL sits.

Now, listen to me. I've got a daughter, called Yvonne, about the same age as you. And I would dearly like to hope that in a similar situation to this, she'd behave the same as you. She'd stay loyal to her mum or myself and be prepared to stand by us. Even offer to take the blame. I'd like to hope she'd behave the same as you. But I very much doubt it. Because despite the fact that she could not have had two more doting, caring, loving parents than my wife and myself, Yvonne is an out-of-control teenage tearaway, who's been in and out of the juvenile courts since she was ten years old. Whereas you, who have a mother with the morals of a large black rat and who quite clearly doesn't give a toss for anyone, who's quite happy to conduct her filthy, sordid business right in her own front room, she ends up with a daughter like you. Well, all I can say is, there is no bloody justice. Mandy, you do not deserve her, you do not deserve this caring, considerate, wonderful child! If it was in my power, I would have her taken away from you right now.

He moves to the door, suddenly weary.

What a world! What a world, eh, Grace?

GRACE "For that which befalleth the sons of men befalleth beasts; even one thing befalleth them; as the one dieth, so dieth the other; yea, they have all one breath; so that a man hath no pre-eminence above a beast; for all is vanity."

DAN I knew you'd have a word for it, Grace. Come on, then. Leave them to it.

He opens the front door.

(In the doorway) This case is still open. We will be watching you like a proverbial hawk, Mandy. You flash even so much as a kneecap anywhere on my patch again and I'll have you. All right? 'Evening.

DAN *goes out.*

GRACE *makes to follow. She turns in the doorway.*

GRACE *(to* SORREL*)* You may have fooled him but you don't fool me, dear. Either of you. We'll catch up with you, don't worry. "So it shall be at the end of the world: the angels shall come forth, and sever the wicked from among the just, and shall cast them into the furnace of fire: there shall be wailing and gnashing of teeth." Merry Christmas.

GRACE *goes out, closing the door.*

Silence.

LYNETTE *(at length, disbelievingly)* Oh, Sorrel.

SORREL I was only... *(Slight pause)* I just was trying to... *(Slight pause)* I only thought it might... *(Slight pause)* You know.

LYNETTE *(softly)* Oh, Sorrel. What have you done to us?

A suddenly agitated ringing of the doorbell.

(wearily) Oh, God. Now what?

SORREL I'll get it. *(She goes to the front door and opens it)*

KELLY *is standing outside in a state of total panic.*

KELLY *(swiftly, panicked)* Sorrel, there's a police car outside. I've just seen it. The police are here. What are we going to do? They must have found out. They know what we did. They must— *(She sees* **LYNETTE** *sitting there)* Oh. *(She realizes)* Oh. *(To* **SORREL***)* Oh, sorry. *(To them both)* Sorry.

They remain isolated in their own thoughts, as the lights fade to blackout.

Scene Three

The same. Three weeks later.

The Christmas tree has gone. Instead there are packing cases, most of them full, stacked in both the kitchen and the living-room. The small items, previously dotted about, have now gone. Everything is packed up for an imminent move.

SORREL *is wrapping some final glasses in newspaper.* KELLY *sits and watches her. They are both very subdued.*

Silence.

KELLY *(at length)* Where exactly is Doncaster, anyway?

SORREL I don't know. *(She indicates vaguely)* Somewhere up there. Yorkshire.

KELLY That's miles away.

SORREL Yep.

KELLY I'll never see you, will I?

SORREL Probably not.

KELLY Yorkshire? They don't even talk the same as us.

SORREL Tell me about it.

KELLY Why did she want to go to Doncaster?

SORREL She used to know some people who lived there.

KELLY Used to know them?

SORREL They're not there any more. They've retired to Spain. Somewhere like that.

KELLY Then why does she want to live in Doncaster?

SORREL *(impatiently)* I don't know.

KELLY Sorry.

Pause.

SORREL It's near Doncaster.

KELLY Ah.

SORREL Not even Doncaster.

KELLY I'll never see you again, will I? Ever?

SORREL Don't know. Shouldn't think so.

KELLY *(in utter despair)* Oh.

She clutches hold of **SORREL** *and clasps her tight.*

SORREL *(a little embarrassed)* Kell, I'm trying to pack.

KELLY *(muffled, still holding* **SORREL***)* I love you.

SORREL Yes. I love you too, Kell. *(Gently)* Now let go. Come on. I have to do this.

KELLY *(releasing her)* Why do you need to go? Why?

SORREL Kell, come on. How can we stay? Everybody's heard. That policeman must have published it in the *Police Gazette*. Mum's had this terrible row with the managing agents. Accusing her of turning the place into a brothel. Half the neighbours aren't talking to us. Kids at school picking on me.

KELLY Only the wankers.

SORREL Well, the school is full of wankers, then.

Pause.

KELLY My mum says I shouldn't talk to you.

SORREL There you are, then.

KELLY I told her she could get stuffed.

SORREL You did?

KELLY Well. I felt like saying it.

Pause.

Where's your mum gone?

SORREL To the shops. If they don't refuse to serve her. She didn't even bother to fight for that job, you know. She just gave up. Rolled over. They were supposed to be Christians. Religious. Pass me that paper, would you?

KELLY *(handing over the paper)* I'm going to miss you so much.

SORREL Don't keep on saying that, Kell. It doesn't help. It really doesn't. I'll miss you.

KELLY Really?

SORREL Yes, I said.

KELLY Really? Really? Really?

SORREL *(going to the bedroom)* Yes!

SORREL goes off.

The front doorbell rings.

(offstage) Answer that, would you?

KELLY answers the door nervously.

It is TROY, a man in his thirties. He wears a thick overcoat and an old college scarf.

TROY *(chirpily)* Hallo, darling. Is your mum at home?

KELLY Who?

TROY Your mum. Is she at home?

KELLY Who wants to know?

TROY I do.

KELLY Who are you?

TROY My name's Troy. Troy Stephens. Can I see your mum? Is she in?

KELLY My mum's—

SORREL enters from the bedroom. She sees TROY.

TROY *(seeing SORREL)* Ah! Hallo there. Just enquiring if her mum's at home.

SORREL Oh, yes? And who are you?

TROY Troy Stephens. I'm from *As It Is*.

SORREL *As It Is?*

TROY As in, Telling It As It Is.

SORREL Yes?

TROY Magazine.

SORREL Really?

TROY Haven't you read it?

SORREL No.

TROY It's very, very popular.

SORREL Is it? That's probably why I haven't read it. What did you want?

TROY I would appreciate a quick word, that's all.

SORREL With her mother?

TROY If it's not too much trouble.

SORREL OK. *(She pauses)* Fire ahead.

TROY How do you mean?

SORREL I'm her mother. Fire ahead.

KELLY suppresses a giggle.

TROY What?

SORREL I'm her mother. Carry on.

TROY You're not her mother.

SORREL Yes, I am.

TROY You can't be.

SORREL Why not?

TROY Well, you're too young.

SORREL Funny. Everyone says that.

TROY Come on. She's not your daughter.

SORREL Am I your mother, Doris?

KELLY Of course you are, Mum.

SORREL There.

TROY Come on!

KELLY Why won't he believe you, Mum?

SORREL I don't know, Doris, nobody does these days.

KELLY What a terrible world, Mum.

SORREL You can say that again, Doris. *(To* TROY*)* Was there anything else you wanted, Mr—

TROY Now listen, I know you're winding me up, I know you are. I just want to know if I can have a word with her mother.

SORREL You're having one now.

TROY Oh, leave it out. I'll come back, I'll come back, this is ridiculous— *(He makes to leave)*

SORREL Bye-bye! Nice to have met you. See the man out, Doris, will you?

SORREL *goes back into the bedroom.*

TROY Is she a lunatic or what? Has she escaped from somewhere?

KELLY Ssshh!

TROY What?

KELLY My mother had me when I was very, very young, you see.

TROY What?

KELLY As a consequence, she has this terrible disease.

TROY Disease.

KELLY It's called youthanasia.

TROY Euthanasia. That's killing people.

KELLY No, no, not euthanasia. Youth-anasia. Y-O-U-T-H.

TROY Get off.

KELLY She got stuck at the age of sixteen. She's now forty-eight, actually.

TROY You could well be her daughter, you're madder than she is. I'll call back.

KELLY Do I get a free magazine?

TROY No, you bloody well don't.

KELLY Thank you.

TROY (*opening the front door*) House full of batty kids...

He nearly walks into **LYNETTE**, *who is returning with her shopping.*

Oh. I'm so sorry, excuse me.

LYNETTE Who are you? What are you doing here?

TROY Ah. My name is Troy Stephens. Are you by any chance Mandy Saxon?

LYNETTE No.

TROY Mrs Lynette Saxon, I'm sorry. But formerly Mandy Saxon. I represent *As It Is* – the magazine which caters for the caring and the curious—

LYNETTE Jolly good. Nice to meet you. Now piss off.

TROY Oh, come on. Come on. Be fair.

LYNETTE Fair? Did you say fair?

    SORREL *enters from the bedroom.*

TROY Give me a chance, that's all.

LYNETTE When were you lot ever fair to me? Eh?

SORREL Take it easy, Mum.

LYNETTE Or to my daughter? Go on, get out. Just get out of here.

TROY I think if you'd only hear me out, you might—

LYNETTE *(wheeling on* **KELLY***)* And your bloody mother's just cut me dead on the stairs. Thank her so much from me, won't you?

KELLY I'm sorry. She doesn't mean to - she just—

LYNETTE Oh no, she means to, Kelly. When people do things, they generally mean them. It's called being responsible for your actions. There's no point in excusing them by saying they didn't mean them when they clearly did.

KELLY *(flustered)* All I meant was—

LYNETTE I'm sure the Japanese didn't mean to bomb Pearl Harbour, but they did.

KELLY *(bewildered)* What?

LYNETTE Lee Harvey Oswald never meant to shoot Kennedy, he just happened to pull the trigger—

SORREL Mum—

KELLY What's she talking about?

LYNETTE Hitler didn't mean to invade Poland, did he?

KELLY Poland?

SORREL *(yelling)* Mum! Will you just cool it!

    LYNETTE *stands breathless.*

    (more quietly) Stop taking it out on Kelly, will you?

KELLY *(tearfully)* Excuse me, please. I need to go home now.

KELLY *rushes out of the door, slamming it behind her.*

TROY *watches all this open-mouthed.*

SORREL Honestly!

LYNETTE I'm going to unpack these. Will you get rid of this... *(She indicates* **TROY***)* ...thing, please.

She goes into the kitchen. She has a small coughing fit which prompts her to stop and light a cigarette. She starts to unpack the food.

SORREL *(to* **TROY***)* I think you'd better go. She doesn't want to talk to you. Not at all.

TROY *wavers uncertainly, then makes up his mind.*

TROY *(decisively)* Allow me one minute. One minute. Will you? Please.

Before **SORREL** *can object he goes into the kitchen.* **LYNETTE** *ignores him.*

Mrs. Saxon, I know you don't wish to talk to me, but I'd be so incredibly grateful if you would listen to me for just one minute. That's all I'm asking. One minute.

Silence.

Please.

LYNETTE I should probably phone the police and get them to throw you out of here but, knowing their opinion of me, it would probably take them a week to get here. One minute, then.

TROY My name is Troy Stephens. I am from As *It Is* magazine. We specialize in highlighting issues, sometimes social, sometimes personal, which we feel would be of interest to and engage the concern of our readers.

LYNETTE A gossip mag, you mean.

TROY No, no. Upmarket from that.

LYNETTE Heavens, a gossip mag with no pictures.

TROY I think there's a story here, which if highlighted properly would be of serious concern. Not to put too fine a point on it, here is yourself, who in order to keep her single parent family together was reduced to selling her body. Supplementing that with occasional office-cleaning. A woman who less than ten weeks earlier, had control of a multi-million pound internet business—

LYNETTE Hardly...

TROY —a successful marriage, a beautiful home, a thriving business partnership, a highly promising, academically brilliant daughter—

SORREL Oh, is that what I am?

TROY —and all of that wiped out overnight. What does that say about us? What does that say about the world we're living in? Don't you find that the tiniest bit frightening?

LYNETTE Yes, I find it terrifying. But then it's us you happen to be talking about.

TROY No, I think it's all of us. When you see how thin the crust is on which we're walking...

LYNETTE And you want to put all this in your magazine?

TROY We'd like to serialize.

LYNETTE My life of shame by ex-millionaire call girl.

TROY We don't write like that. Listen. If it's the publicity you dislike – well, you're saying it yourself – you've already got that. At least whatever you say for us, we'd get it right.

LYNETTE Any guarantee of that?

TROY Every guarantee. We'd pay well.

LYNETTE Ah ha! Here it comes. I tell you now, you could never in a million years afford my price. We ex-whores don't come cheap.

TROY I would hope not.

He looks round, cautiously.

Is this the sort of thing you had in mind?

He produces a pen and notepad and scrawls a figure on the top sheet. He shows it to **LYNETTE** *obviously expecting her to be impressed.*

Yes?

LYNETTE *(studying this, deadpan)* Uh-huh. How about...?

She takes the pen from his hand and makes a simple annotation. She hands the pad back.

That's the sort of thing I had in mind.

TROY *(looking at what she's added)* Jesus!

LYNETTE Take it or leave it.

TROY We've never paid that.

LYNETTE If you want me to sell you my soul, I will only do it for the price of my daughter's future. Otherwise why should I bother?

SORREL Mum. What are you doing?

TROY I'd need to make a call.

LYNETTE Do that. It's that or nothing, tell them.

TROY Excuse me. Won't be a second. *(He opens the front door. With an afterthought)* You will let me in again, won't you?

LYNETTE Depends on your answer.

TROY See you in a tick.

TROY goes out, closing the door.

SORREL What are you doing? You don't need to do this?

LYNETTE *(shrugging)* What else have I got to lose?

SORREL You'll be all over his nasty little magazine. We both will.

LYNETTE Three-minute wonder, love. Believe me.

SORREL How much did you ask for?

LYNETTE Enough to widen our options. I added another nought to his offer, that's all.

SORREL Will they pay that much?

LYNETTE Probably not. Worth a go, though. Look, I've got an idea. Whilst he's making his phone call…

She heads for the kitchen.

Have you packed those glasses yet?

SORREL Yes, they're just on the top there.

LYNETTE Well, unwrap them again. Two glasses. Quickly.

SORREL What for?

LYNETTE Quick, quick, quick!

> SORREL *locates the glasses wrapped in newspaper and starts to unpack them.* LYNETTE *goes into the kitchen and opens the fridge.*

SORREL What are you doing?

She unpacks the wine glasses on to the coffee table.

> LYNETTE *returns with the still-unopened bottle of pink champagne.*

LYNETTE Here. We still have this. Left over from our celebratory meal that never was.

SORREL How do we know this is celebratory?

LYNETTE We don't. We wait and see. He'll be back in a minute. If it's no, we'll just have to put this away again, won't we?

Wait for another time. Because there will be another time. I promise you that, Sorrel. I swear to you that this family, you and I, are going to have another time.

The doorbell rings. They freeze.

Here we go, then. Make or break time, darling.

Clutching the bottle, she goes to answer the door. She opens it expectantly.

KELLY *is standing there.*

Oh, no.

KELLY *(defensively)* I'm sorry. I'll go away again.

LYNETTE No, come in, come in. I thought you were...someone else.

KELLY Oh. I'm Kelly.

LYNETTE I know you're Kelly, you stupid girl.

KELLY *steps inside and* **LYNETTE** *closes the door behind her.*

KELLY I just wanted to apologize if I upset you, Mrs Saxon – I didn't mean to—

LYNETTE No, Kelly. I don't believe in this case that you did mean it. I apologize to you. It was entirely me. I had no reason to speak to you like that. None at all. Will you accept my apology? Please.

KELLY Oh.

She stares at **SORREL** *and* **LYNETTE** *with something little short of sheer adoration. She bursts into tears.*

You're such lovely people...

SORREL Now, don't do that, Kelly. There's no need to cry. Here. Unpack yourself a glass.

KELLY A what?

SORREL A glass, there. There's a remote chance we may be drinking.

KELLY Is there? Are you still leaving?

LYNETTE We're not sure. We'll know in a minute.

KELLY *(mystified)* Oh.

SORREL *(comforting her)* I promise, it'll work out fine, Kell, you'll see. *(To* LYNETTE*)* Won't it?

LYNETTE shrugs. The doorbell rings. They all look to the door.

LYNETTE This time it must be. Here goes.

She starts to move to the door.

SORREL Mum...

LYNETTE Mmmm?

SORREL Whatever the outcome—

She hugs her.

LYNETTE *(responding)* Whatever the outcome.

She moves to the door.

Hell, it's only money.

KELLY *(whispering)* What's going on?

SORREL You'll see.

LYNETTE *(her hand on the door handle)* Ready, then? And... one...two...three...

She prepares to throw open the door.

The lights fade swiftly to blackout.

Curtain.

FURNITURE AND PROPERTY LIST

Further dressing may be added at the director's discretion

ACT I

Scene One

Onstage: Bar containing few bottles
Desk. *In drawer:* **Sorrel**'s bag containing mobile phone
Chair
Sofa
Armchair
Heavy coffee table
Healthy pot plants
Small dining table
4 chairs
Hi-fi
CDs
Kettle
Tea bags
2 mugs
Microwave
Lynette's bag containing packet of cigarettes, lighter, mirror
Coat
Fridge containing 2 cans of cola
Biscuit tin containing biscuits

Personal: **Lynette:** wrist-watch
Kelly: backpack
Sorrel: prefect's badge

Scene Two

Set: **Lynette**'s bag on table. *In it:* cigarettes, lighter
Bottle of white wine in fridge
Corkscrew

	2 glasses
	Supper in microwave
Offstage:	Several carrier bags, backpack containing mobile phone (**Sorrel**)

Scene Three

Strike:	Supper plates of food
	Bottle of wine
	Glasses
	Lynette's bag
Offstage:	2 carrier bag containing bottles of alcohol and "girlie" magazines (**Sorrel**)
	Bulky package in chemist's shop bag, high-heeled shoes (**Kelly**)
	Small bunch of flowers (**Leo**)
Personal:	**Leo:** wrist-watch
	Sorrel: wrist-watch

ACT II

Scene One

Strike:	Girlie magazines
Set:	Laptop
	Lynnete's bag containing cigarettes and lighter
	Sorrel's bag containing 2 mobile phones
Offstage:	Heavy object in blanket (**Sorrel** and **Kelly**)
Personal:	**Kelly:** woolen gloves, ski-mask

Scene Two

Set:	Small decorated Christmas tree
	Christmas cards
Offstage:	Mobile phone, backpack containing another (**Sorrel**)
	Carrier bag containing bottle of pink champagne (**Lynette**)

Personal:	**Sorrel:** scarf, hat
	Dan: notebook, pen, scrap of paper, photograph, mobile phone

Scene Three

Strike:	Christmas tree
	Cards
	Small ornaments
Set:	Packing cases
	2 glasses in newspaper
	Unopened bottle of pink champagne
Offstage:	Shopping bags, bag containing cigarettes and lighter (**Lynette**)
Personal:	**Troy:** old college scarf, pen, notepad

LIGHTING PLOT

Property fittings required: nil
1 interior. The same throughout

ACT I, Scene One

To open: Soft yellow glow from outside

Cue 1	**Kelly** waits *Fade to blackout*	(Page 20)

ACT I, Scene Two

To open: Evening lighting

Cue 2	**Lynette** resumes serving up the meal *Fade to blackout*	(Page 27)

ACT I, Scene Three

To open: Early afternoon lighting

Cue 3	**Sorrel**: "Oh, God." *Blackout*	(Page 49)

ACT II, Scene One

To open: Evening lighting

Cue 4	**Sorrel** switches off lights at the door *Snap off lights, bring up effect of boat passing outside*	(Page 54)
Cue 5	**Sorrel** and **Kelly** laugh *Fade to blackout*	(Page 59)

ACT II, Scene Two

To open: Darkness

Cue 6	**Sorrel** switches on the lights *Snap on lights*	(Page 60)

Cue 7   **Kelly**: "Sorry."   (Page 79)
         Fade to blackout

ACT II, Scene Three

To open: Overall general lighting

Cue 8   **Lynette** prepares to throw open the door   (Page 92)
         Fade swiftly to blackout

EFFECTS PLOT

ACT I

Cue 1	**Sorrel** dries mugs *Doorbell rings*	(Page 9)
Cue 2	**Lynette** lights cigarette on balcony *Sound of party boat passing, loud beat music and laughter*	(Page 21)
Cue 3	**Sorrel**: "Would I do that, Mother?" *Mobile phone rings*	(Page 25)
Cue 4	**Sorrel**: "...a bit disgusting, actually, that's why..." *Sound of party boat passing noisily*	(Page 25)
Cue 5	**Sorrel** starts to unpack bottles *Doorbell rings*	(Page 28)
Cue 6	Room is empty for a moment *Doorbell rings*	(Page 33)
Cue 7	**Sorrel**: "Sshh!" *Doorbell rings*	(Page 33)
Cue 8	**Kelly**: "...should have got the bigger size." *Doorbell rings*	(Page 34)
Cue 9	**Sorrel**: "Not all at once." *Doorbell rings*	(Page 34)
Cue 10	**Kelly** starts playing CD *Easy-listening music*	(Page 35)
Cue 11	**Kelly** turns up the volume (2 cues) *Turn up the volume*	(Page 48)
Cue 12	**Kelly** switches off CD player *Cut music*	(Page 48)
Cue 13	**Sorrel** closes laptop *Mobile rings in **Sorrel**'s bag*	(Page 54)

Cue 14	**Sorrel** switches off lights *Sound of party boat passing*	(Page 54)
Cue 15	**Sorrel** and **Kelly** throw object over rail *Object hitting water effect*	(Page 58)
Cue 16	**Dan** makes call *After a moment, phone rings in* **Lynette**'s *bag*	(Page 73)

Cue 17	**Dan**: "Do we hear anything or
	    don't we?"
	After a moment, **Sorrel**'s *mobile rings*
	    in desk drawer
		(Page 74)

Cue 18	**Lynnete**: "What have you done to us?" *Agitated ringing of doorbell*	(Page 79)
Cue 19	**Sorrel** goes off *Doorbell rings*	(Page 82)
Cue 20	**Lynette**: "...are going to have another time." *Doorbell rings*	(Page 91)
Cue 21	**Lynette** shrugs *Doorbell rings*	(Page 92)

THIS IS NOT THE END

Visit samuelfrench.co.uk and discover the best theatre bookshop on the internet

A vast range of plays
Acting and theatre books
Gifts

samuelfrench.co.uk
samuelfrenchltd
samuel french uk

www.ingramcontent.com/pod-product-compliance
Ingram Content Group UK Ltd.
Pitfield, Milton Keynes, MK11 3LW, UK
UKHW021843210426
5322IPUK00022B/442